THE WELFARE WORLD

THE WELFARE WORLD

By

REED K. CLEGG

Director, Fresno County Department of Public Welfare
Assistant Professor of Criminology
Fresno State College
Fresno, California

CHARLES C THOMAS · PUBLISHER
Springfield · Illinois · U.S.A.

Published and Distributed Throughout the World by

CHARLES C THOMAS · PUBLISHER

BANNERSTONE HOUSE

301-327 East Lawrence Avenue, Springfield, Illinois, U.S.A.

NATCHEZ PLANTATION HOUSE

735 North Atlantic Boulevard, Fort Lauderdale, Florida, U.S.A.

With THOMAS BOOKS *careful attention is given to all details of
manufacturing and design. It is the Publisher's desire to present books
that are satisfactory as to their physical qualities and artistic possibilities
and appropriate for their particular use.* THOMAS BOOKS *will be true
to those laws of quality that assure a good name and good will.*

Printed in the United States of America

8-K

To My Sister
Lula

Preface

PUBLIC WELFARE affects the lives of millions of Americans, and its programs require the expenditure of billions of tax dollars. While the average citizen has expected public assistance to decrease and disappear, its growth has been spectacular.

In spite of the magnitude of welfare, it has remained a mystery to those who benefit from it and to those whose tax dollars support it. With age and growth the programs which provide for the needy have become a vast riddle of regulations and a dense jungle of technical complexity.

Those who receive assistance see only their immediate personal problems. Those whose tax bills are earmarked for welfare fail to comprehend its intricacies. In substitution for knowledge, tales of fantasy are draped over back yard fences and wound around social gatherings.

Those who view welfare from afar see dishonesty, immorality, and indolence. An intimate acquaintance with the needy discloses the fact that they are, by and large, a cross section of American life. They are aged and young, disabled and healthy. Among them are the honest and the dishonest, the lazy and the ambitious, in about the same ratio to be found in the nonrecipient population. In the main they are the victims of a social and economic system which has passed them by. In a highly industrialized society they are the unskilled and uneducated. In the shadows of the welfare office they participate numbly in the daily dramas of life, death, humor and pathos which are a part of the welfare world.

Public assistance has been a part of society since the dawn of history. In one form or another it will continue to be an increasingly important part of our economic structure. Only as we accept this fact and as we become cognizant of the social and economic phenomena which spawn the need for public assistance will we begin to formulate solutions to the welfare problem.

The right to privacy is a precious American heritage. Names and circumstances in *The Welfare World* have been disguised and blended to insure the preservation of individual human dignity, the rightful heritage of those who are recipients of public assistance.

REED K. CLEGG

Contents

THE WELFARE WORLD

Chapter I

A Day To Remember

PUBLIC WELFARE operates in a world of its own. It is concerned with masses of people and millions of dollars. The welfare recipient, like the proverbial tree in the forest, sees only his own personal situation. Those outside the realm of welfare see flashes of a confusing and disturbing picture which features fraud, indolence and irresponsibility.

Inside the welfare office there is a sense of urgency uncommon to other government offices. Change and confusion are constant companions and the atmosphere is much more conducive to ulcers than it is to rust. The welfare employee gets tired, angry, frustrated and disgusted. He does not get bored because the recipients and the taxpayers will not leave him alone long enough for that state of mind to set in.

There are always things undone at the day's end and each morning brings its own new problems. There are no two days which are ever alike. One day in particular, however, stands out in my memory. It started out like many other days, with a rash of calls from the unhappy, the dissatisfied and the disgruntled. About half of the calls were from recipients of aid, would-be recipients, their relatives and an assortment of do-gooders. The general theme was that there was not enough welfare and that I was the chief architect of starvation and want. One unhappy recipient informed me that I was driving a Cadillac and eating caviar while she was walking and eating oatmeal. It just happens that I drive a Corvair and that oatmeal cereal is one of my favorites, and I have yet to eat caviar.

An acquaintance called who is noted for his conservative stand

3

on most issues and on welfare in particular. It seems that a neighbor of his had been denied Old Age Assistance. He recited her virtues to me: she had been a long-time resident of our city, a prominent club member and a taxpayer for sixty years. It was impossible for my conservative friend to understand how we were helping "all those bums and winos" and would refuse to help her. I attempted to explain to him that welfare was granted or denied on the basis of circumstances and not on the degree of virtue or the length of time as a taxpayer. I mentioned that a certain madam with a long history of successful management of a house of ill fame had applied on the same date as his neighbor, was found to be eligible and would receive a monthly old-age security grant. My line of reasoning was completely unacceptable to him and our conversation only further convinced him that welfare was designed only for bums, winos and prostitutes and that somehow I was personally determined to underwrite immorality.

The other half of the calls came from that broad classification of citizens who call themselves taxpayers. This term is anything but exclusive—it also includes kids, bums, winos and women of questionable virtue—but some people regard it as a small exclusive group of which they are charter members. According to my taxpaying friends there was altogether too much welfare, and my employees and I were determined to sink the economy and to encourage the increase of that portion of the population which refuses to work. There is never a day when telephone calls of this kind do not come in. If any welfare director were at his desk and did not get more or less of a steady patter of them, he would suspect that his telephone was out of order.

This particular day had all the appearances of being a very gloomy one. It had been raining steadily for more than three weeks. The farm laborers were unable to work, and they had come to our department for help. The day before, we had assisted nine hundred families and this day would see well over a thousand come through our doors. They were large families with an average of seven children each, and they presented a picture of gloom and deprivation. They were wet, their clothes were soiled, and the odor in our waiting room was indicative of their lack of bathing and other sanitary facilities; but they were remarkably cheerful and courteous. There was no crowding or shoving but an amazing display of patience as they stood in long lines under a steady downpour. Our waiting room would accommodate only a part of them, and while we utilized garages and all other available shelter, many of them stood in the rain rather than risk getting out of place in the line for groceries.

A trip to the welfare department even under the most adverse circumstances is a family affair for many farm workers and seems to carry with it some air of celebration. Although either the father or mother can apply and receive help, the family comes as a unit. Many of the children who were there on that day were barefooted, and while this distressed us, the children were having an unusual amount of fun as they ran through the rain puddles and splashed water on each other. We have tried for years to discourage these family pilgrimages, particularly because they take the children out of school and because they overcrowd our facilities, but we have failed completely in this effort. There must be some reason why they make a family affair out of it: it may be that their lives are so routine and devoid of recreation that a trip to the welfare department is an excursion. Some sharp advertising executive might dream up a slogan to the effect that the family that applies together, stays together, but I doubt that this would be descriptive of the reasons why the kids come with their parents.

I had reason for some real concern about the situation in which we found ourselves on that particular morning. Our workers had been going at a terrific pace for more than three weeks. They had come early, worked late and had been cutting their lunch hour in half. They were tired and they looked it. I wondered how much longer they could stand up under the strain. In addition to the work involved there is something about seeing large numbers of hungry people which does something to one's soul and body. One cannot help but feel a little bit guilty about the fact that he has a comfortable home, warm clothing and plenty to eat.

Most of the food which we were distributing was Federal surplus from the Department of Agriculture. It came in bulk and had to be broken down into family allotments according to "guide lines" issued by the Department. We had been working Saturdays and Sundays to package beans, rice, flour and other commodities, and part of our help for this operation came from county jail prisoners who were on loan to us during the daytime. We had been running low on supplies of surplus food, but the State Department of Education, which delivers the Federal surplus food to us, had brought in thirty-five tons that morning and had unloaded it before nine o'clock.

In the middle of all this we had been engaged in a running battle with the bureaucracy of the Department of Agriculture. One of the surplus food items was canned meat and gravy. This was a particularly good product, since it was very well prepared and nutritious and could be warmed over an open fire or wired to a car exhaust with equally satisfactory results. With the rain coming down in a never-ending deluge, and with hundreds of families in and around our facilities, the Department of Agriculture ordered us to return all the canned meat we had on hand. There were several hundred cases in our warehouse and we were going to need every bit of it. The Federal order specified that cases which had been opened would not need to be returned. It did not take us long to open all the cases we had and we kept right on issuing canned meat.

The San Francisco office of the Department of Agriculture required us to keep a strict inventory. They knew we had a lot of canned meat on hand and when it did not come back to them in compliance with their order they sent the office manager down to see what had happened. The office manager was a very reasonable person and he saw our predicament, but he had his orders from Washington and told us to send the canned meat back. We had reached the point of desperation; we could not provide proper food for several thousand hungry persons without the canned meat and we were determined to keep it at all costs, including the risk of defying the Federal government. I told the office manager that we would not return the meat short of a Federal court order. He called his boss in Washington and put me on the line to him, and I told him the same thing. The Washington "boss" said he would have to take it up with the Secretary of Agriculture and that we would be hearing from him. Our San Francisco friend advised us as he left that an order from Washington was indeed an order and he would suggest that we start loading the canned meat. The next morning he called us from San Francisco to say that it was completely beyond his understanding and that it had never occurred before but that we could keep the meat and distribute it to our hungry families.

I was so depressed and discouraged that I felt I had to get away from the office for awhile, even though I had twinges of conscience about leaving the rest of the employees to face the situation. There was a report luncheon downtown that day for a summary of the annual charity drive of a number of community agencies. As I walked down a main street it was if I had stepped into a completely different world. Well-dressed people, with raincoats and umbrellas were in a festive mood. Many of them were shopping for Christmas and their arms were loaded with gaily wrapped packages. On the curb in front of one of our largest banks, a middle-aged man sat in all the rain with nothing to shelter him but an old and very soggy raincoat. He was opening a package of surplus food which had been recently issued from our commissary and was devouring a handful of raisins. Amidst all the evident gaiety and wealth he was the sole reminder of that other world which I had left—the world of wet and hungry people crowded together in a garage, patiently awaiting their turn to be issued some of the necessities of life; the world where tired and discouraged eyes peered out from a mass of damply pressed bodies; the world where barefooted children ran laughing through rain puddles—the welfare world.

Two fashionably dressed women approached from the opposite direction. They were disconcerted by the sight of the man eating on the curb and I heard one of them remark, "Why do they allow this kind of thing? These people should be made to stay over on the West Side."

The report luncheon was held in a large auditorium. It featured a film which had been produced locally and which opened with scenes of the valley, the vast mountains to the east and the jagged range on the west. The narrator described it as the beautiful and wonderfully productive valley it is. He mentioned the mild winter climate of the valley and the snowy playland of the mountains. I had been able to enjoy all this but when he described the valley as a peaceful place without problems, particularly economic fluctuations associated with climate, I realized that I worked in an entirely different world. The world of downtown knew little of the welfare world. It celebrated and congratulated itself on its lack of problems while less than a mile way the barefoot children and their hungry parents stood in line for surplus commodities.

When I returned to the welfare department I had to thread my way through crowds of people who, unmindful of the rain, were queued up in long winding lines, one end of which emerged from a garage, and the other terminated in a crowded waiting room with mud on the floor but a secure roof overhead. A middle-aged and rather large woman approached me and in a voice which rang loud and clear inquired, "Are you the welfare director?" When I replied in the affirmative, she said, "You're the one who has all our money in your pocket while we go hungry. You cut my check five dollars last month, and you've got my money."

Her remarks drew a lot of attention and I was more than startled. I attempted to explain to her that the amount she received was determined by law and that I could not take money from her and keep it myself. This attempted explanation was completely ineffectual, and she repeated her original charge with renewed vigor and volume. I finally told her that if she had evidence that I had wrongfully taken any money, she should contact the district attorney and sign a complaint against me. She did not want any part of this procedure but continued to reiterate her charges.

At that time we had a deputy district attorney in our department who was a most eager prosecutor. I went to his office and asked him to accompany me to the yard. We had no difficulty locating my accuser, who was still holding forth to a large and interested audience. I introduced the deputy district attorney and said, "This woman has accused me of taking money which doesn't belong to me. I ask that you have her file a complaint against me." The deputy demanded that the woman file a complaint but she refused. His anger rose, and he threatened to file charges against her for making a false accusation. She left us and pushed her way through the crowd, some of whom heckled her in rather ungentle terms.

When I got back in my office my secretary had two messages for me. The weatherman was still predicting continued rain, and

Jim, one of our social workers, wanted to see me on what he had said was a most urgent matter. Jim was a handsome young man with a definite appeal to the opposite sex. He had been with us less than a year and I wondered what was bringing him to my office on an urgent matter. When he entered there was no doubt about the state of his anxiety. He looked around the room and at the doorway through which he had just entered as if he expected someone to follow him. "I have to leave work right away," he said. I thought he had some immediate errand to run and told him that I thought it could be arranged. "You don't understand," he said, "I have to get out of town." I mentioned our usual two weeks' notice on resignations and said that I would be sorry to see him leave. "I can't give two weeks notice; I have to get out of town tonight."

He was so agitated that I did not attempt to question him further. He left the office and from acquaintances I learned that he left town immediately. To this day I do not know whether he was the center of a triangle or just what prompted his hasty exit, but I have always thought there was a member of the fair sex involved in some manner.

Jim's resignation was one of many we had received that month, and as I reflected on our persistent personnel problems I could not help but think of the frequent accusation that we purposely increased our staff to "build an empire." While this belief is rather widespread, it has to come from those who have never hired or supervised many employees. There is an adage among executives that more employees bring more headaches. This is so true that anyone with experience will employ the minimum number of people necessary to do the job in order to save the wear and tear on himself. With a large staff of employees, someone is always in trouble. When the number of people on the payroll exceeds the number of those one can remember and call by name, the job assumes an impersonal quality which takes a lot of satisfaction out of it.

This was brought to my mind in a rather forcible manner recently when I met one of our newest employees wandering down a hallway. He did not recognize me and I could not recall his name but I did remember employing him a few days before. He was a young man with few compunctions and as I approached he greeted me with, "Say, what the hell goes on around here anyway?" I told him that I did not know but asked him to come and let me know when he found out. He inquired as to where he could find me, and when I told him I was usually in the director's office, he was not visibly perturbed.

On another occasion we had hired a number of people to help interview an unusually large number of applicants. Somewhat in the manner of the taxicab counterattack which saved Paris in World War I, we had thrown them into the situation with nothing more than a brief explanation as to what was expected of them. I had gone out to an adjacent building where the new employees had been stationed, and pushed and squeezed my way through a crowded waiting room. As I came near an inner door, one of the young men we had employed that morning opened it and called out the name of an applicant for aid who was somewhere in the room. As I stepped towards the open door he grabbed my hand in a most friendly fashion, pumped it a couple of times and informed me that he had my application and hoped he could be of assistance to me. I told him that I was the director of the department and that I was doubtful that the taxpayers would approve of my making an application for welfare aid. This upset his equilibrium so thoroughly that in the interests of the department it might have been better to have sent him home for the rest of the day.

Sometime after five o'clock I decided to go home but I wanted to take a look at things in the commissary first. There was a long line of people waiting, and since the men in the commissary had been working steadily from seven o'clock that morning, I felt obligated to try to help. They were so busy that it was difficult to get one of them to talk with me, but when I offered to assist them I was told that there was a bottleneck at the window where the groceries were issued and that maybe I could help the fellow there. My partner at the window looked at me with less than a vote of confidence in his gaze but I took off my coat and listened to his brief explanation of standard operating procedures at the window. He was a large-boned man with muscle rippling under his county jail uniform and I recognized him as one of our "winter perannuals." In the summer he was a logger in the high Sierras, but when the snow came it left time on his hands, and he imbibed too freely and became a guest at our local pokey. A model prisoner, he was always a trustee, much under demand by county departments. There was nothing I could seem to do to please him. He informed me that I was slow and awkward and of little use. I went along with him, answered him courteously and tried to follow his directions. Operations inside the commissary, meanwhile, were considerably slowed as everyone peeked out the window to observe my partner taking me to task. We worked together for two hours and never once in all that time did I do anything to please him. When we finally finished I went to get my coat and he rather grudgingly admitted that I had tried hard but that I was the slowest and most awkward man he had ever worked with.

As I walked away, one of our regular employees asked my partner if he knew who I was. He said "no" but that he hoped I did not ever come back to help him again. They told him I was the "big boss," and he was shaken for a minute, but I do not think it changed his opinion of me as a helper. Although we have had some busy days at the commissary since then, the boys out there have not seemed to need my help—at least they have not asked for it.

I went home, ate very little and fell into bed at an unusually early hour. Sometime in the early morning hours I awoke to sense that something was different. The rain which had been pounding on the roof for weeks had ceased. I got up and looked out the window at a clear sky. The next morning the sun came out and a very wet world was venting clouds of steam but was already in the drying-up process. The sun shone steadily for the next several days and our reception room became less crowded as the farm laborers returned to the fields. Once again they had demonstrated that they were willing to work when work was available. They are one of the most maligned groups of which I know and are frequently referred to as "lazy bums" and other less endearing terms. Actually they possess a remarkable degree of independence.

Most of them prefer farm labor with all its drawbacks. They are in many respects the nearest to rugged individualists that we have left in this country.

Many years have passed since that rainy day. A program of aid to the unemployed now makes special concessions to the farm workers by labeling them *part-time employees* regardless of what hours they work. Under this designation some of them have lost their former independence. It may be that most of them will be in the mainstream of dependence before too long. If this happens, it is our fault, not theirs, for they wanted work and we provided them with welfare.

Most people I know tell me that they sleep deeply and untroubled when the rain falls on the roof at night. I do not do so well, for I am prone to remember long lines of damp bodies waiting for food and barefoot children running in the rain. It may be that even at night when the rain comes down I am still a captive of the welfare world.

Chapter II

The Inevitable Question

Gee, I wish I had that much money every month to take home to *my* wife and kids. How can I get on welfare?" The scene was not in a ghetto of the poor, nor was this question asked in the crowded waiting room of a welfare department. Rather it was posed in the dining room of a plush hotel where the poor rarely, if ever, dined. The mysteries of public welfare were being explored in a service club setting. It was a noon luncheon with the usual fine-levying and other frivolities engaged in during the weekly session by harassed businessmen anxious to get away from it all for a few minutes.

One of the extracurricular activities of welfare department employees is to speak before service groups. This can be both a rewarding and a frustrating experience, depending upon the circumstances and the setting. I had been asked to speak about welfare to a service club, most of whose members were young businessmen. In general they were men in their thirties and forties who had inherited their fathers' establishments and continued on in the family tradition. I knew most of their fathers and I was acquainted with the majority of them. Although I have done a great deal of public speaking under some difficult and controversial situations, I had some apprehension about facing this group.

Speaking before service clubs is a difficult task. After the festivities and the luncheon and the business items are disposed of, there remains a period of twenty to thirty minutes in which the speaker is supposed to explain all the intricacies of the vast and complicated welfare system and in addition answer a multitude of pointed and quite frequently hostile questions.

This group looked like it could be a little more difficult to handle than some others. These young men were, in company with all other adults and many children in our population, taxpayers. They were more acutely conscious of taxes than most groups because the expenses of conducting government represented a direct business expense to them. No one likes taxes, and since welfare and taxes are synonymous in most people's minds, anyone attempting to explain expenditures for public welfare programs can expect varying amounts of curiosity or outright hostility.

In addition to considering themselves overburdened taxpayers, these young men had other important self-styled distinctions. They were primarily self-made men and secondarily rugged individualists. The fact that their fathers' retirement ages coincided with their attainment of majority was something they either did not think about or submerged such thoughts as not being compatible with their present status. Their sires had pioneered and developed established business firms and had passed the ready-made product on to their sons. This too was something to be forgotten in their smug acceptance of the "self-made man" image.

The usual peas, carrots and roast beef menu mingled with the butterflies in my stomach with uncertain results. The preliminaries were concluded and I assumed the responsibilities of speaker of the day. How does one tell about a conglomerate of programs, each with its own set of rules and regulations—regulations, the sum total of which are contained in several volumes of finely printed material phrased by masters in the art of bureaucratic gobbledygook? It is not easy; at the end of twenty minutes one has skipped from rim to rim of a Grand Canyon of complexity with the feeling that the seeds of confusion have been sown.

The question-and-answer period extends over a time of approximately ten minutes with a forest of upraised hands and questions which should be the subject matter of a half-hour's explanation and which must be answered in a few seconds. There are some favorite questions which always arise. There are always some new ones and some which one does not expect. There is usually the inevitable question from the would-be clown, "How can I get on welfare?" It is always good for a round of belly laughs. The members of this particular club had one consuming interest: they wanted to know how much a family with dependent children could receive from welfare, and as I read off the maximum monthly payments—which ranged from $145.00 for one child up to $401.00 for fourteen—they were busy with pencil and paper. When I finished there was a near-unanimous chorus of "Gee, I wish I could take that much home to *my* wife and kids every month."

I have been around welfare departments in an official capacity for some fifteen years. During that period of time I have spoken to groups whose combined totals would number many thousands. I have talked to the far right and the extreme left and I have been heckled by experts, but never before had I been dumbfounded and rendered speechless. The majority of my audience was in the $10,000 to $12,000 annual income bracket. They had purchased new homes, drove modern automobiles, and some of them flew their own airplanes, yet here they were pretending to envy the plight of welfare recipients and in effect asking the inevitable question, "How can I get on welfare?" It took me a few minutes to recover and when I did I lost some of my composure and replied in kind. The implied suggestion that I would believe that they really wanted to change circumstances with welfare recipients and that they would be interested in assuming the status of a welfare family engendered a rather pointed reply: I told them that I was aware of their approximate financial position and that I could not believe they really wanted to exchange places with those on welfare. I told them that the first time they brought home nothing more than a welfare family receives they would find themselves parties to a number of divorce actions. Several years have passed, and for some strange reason I have not been invited back to speak to that particular club.

"How can I get on welfare?" is the question most frequently asked of those who are employees of public welfare departments. The question is asked at all hours of the day and night, under any and all circumstances and by all kinds of people. It overshadows all other queries about public welfare, whose essential features appear to most people to be clouded in mystery and founded upon principles which they fail to comprehend. If they do understand they usually oppose, rather vigorously, certain provisions which affect either them personally or some "case" they know about.

The inevitable question comes not only from the economically deprived in our society but from all levels, including the influential and the affluent. It is not too difficult to determine why the question comes from a person of limited financial resources: he may, because of his conditions and circumstances, be entitled to assistance, or he may be a mere step above the thin borderline which sometimes separates those who get public assistance and those who do not. The intricacies of the law are a puzzle to him. He sees only his own needs and desires and does not understand what prevents their fulfillment.

Frequently he sees the interviewer, the caseworker or the agency executive as the real block to his aspirations. They do not like him, or they are more favorably inclined towards aiding someone else of a different race, religion, national origin or political affiliation. To him the question is of vital importance; he envisions a possible improvement in his economic status and a secure future and is concerned as to how it can be obtained. The blocking of his desires adds nothing to his feelings about public welfare in general and its employees in particular.

The deserted wife with minor children may make inquiry as a solution to an immediate and sometimes desperate situation. If her physically departed husband failed to provide the necessities of life but regularly assisted her in becoming pregnant, as so often is the case, she may be under the urgent necessity of obtaining food and shelter for a brood of minor children. For reasons as yet undetermined by sociologists, those who fail to provide for minor children are frequently those who are most ambitious in the role of producing them.

How to get on welfare and how to exist on it after one makes the grade is a shocking experience for the wife and mother of the departed husband and father who has provided a comfortable living. The near-affluent nonworking spouse frequently has visions of public assistance as a comfortable existence and is surprised and upset by its meager financial rewards. The intake function at any welfare department is familiar with the considerable percentage of applicants for aid to dependent children who are quickly disillusioned in the early stages of the application process and who drop out, not to be seen again at the welfare office. What happens to them, where they go and what they do would be the subject of a most interesting study. It is known that some of them in the process of divorce suddenly decide that there are worse situations than an incompatible husband. How many find some means of self-support? How many move in with relatives? How many accept the support of a common-law relationship? These are interesting questions. The answers, however, cannot be found in welfare departments.

Recently a woman in her early thirties appeared in our waiting room to make application for aid. Her husband left on a "business trip" and failed to return. There was another woman in the picture, and the expenses involved in supporting the eternal triangle had severely strained family finances. The husband, in fact, left his legal wife little other than an accumulation of debts and two preschool children. She knew nothing of welfare, had never been employed and was, as she aptly described herself, a "babe in the woods." Her expectations of welfare were far beyond what she could realize from it. As she struggled through the question-and-answer process involved in applying for assistance she became more and more disillusioned.

First of all she was told that she could not even make formal application for a cash grant of aid until her husband had been gone ninety days. The fact that the legislature in its attempt to cure the "weekend-father racket" had established this provision did not exactly fit her situation. The crowning blow was the realization that when the ninety days had expired and aid had been approved she would receive the sum of $168.00 per month. The $6,000 annual salary of her husband, while it had been shared with her rival, provided her with much more than she would receive from welfare.

She was in a state of tears and shock and, as so often is the case, demanded to see someone higher up in the ladder of authority. She came into my office with two precocious but frightened children clinging to her and between sobs talked about the impossibilities of her situation.

"I simply cannot live on $168.00 per month," she said. "What am I to do? Do I steal, become a prostitute or give my children away?" Unfortunately I had little to offer in the way of helpful suggestions other than the fact that this was all the law allowed for two children and that many women and children in our city were living on a similar amount. She left the office and has never returned to complete her application. In doing so she joined the ranks of those who needed help but could not accept the drastic reduction in standards of living which getting on welfare frequently requires.

At times like these I am prone to think of my own family under circumstances which would necessitate their applying for welfare. It is anything but a comforting thought, and I sometimes wonder if the affluent young businessman ever actually imagines his family in the same circumstances. I have been in and around welfare departments for many years, but I have yet to meet the seasoned welfare worker who would seriously ask the question, "How can I get on welfare?"

Why do people ask such a question? Is it always in jest or is envy involved? Why do the affluent pretend to envy the plight of the poor? I have a friend who explains it this way: he says that there is in all Americans a desire to receive something for nothing and that when we see someone else achieving this we envy them, regardless of the circumstances. He points to a situation in a club where we are members as an example of this phase of American philosophy. On occasion our club dinner is served without charge and attendance is at a maximum—in fact, we see members we have not greeted since the last free dinner. This, says my friend, is due to the fact that they, too, want something for nothing.

Regardless of the reasons why some people inquire about getting on welfare, it will always remain a mystery to those of us who know welfare intimately. After a day in the welfare office with all its problems, its frustrations and its pressures, we retreat to the security of our homes, offering prayers of gratitude for not being on welfare and hoping that neither we nor those near to us well ever have to complete the formal process which seriously poses the question, "Can I get on welfare?"

It is true that there are those who ask the question in real seriousness and to whom the answer is all-important. There are some few who exert herculean efforts to achieve the status of a welfare recipient and who, if they applied the same energy and ingenuity in productive pursuits, could join the ranks of the affluent and make the inquiry at a service club luncheon. Herb was one of these. He did have a sight problem, but he was bent on convincing the welfare department that he was legally blind. Legal blindness, incidentally, is not necessarily total loss of sight. Anyone who has lost 98 per cent of his vision is usually conceded to be blind and if he fulfills other requirements can become a recipient of aid to the blind. Herb carried a white cane and sometimes tapped it inquiringly in front of him. When no one was near he looped it over his arm and went on his way with a confident stride. He had applied many times and had been rejected on an equal number of occasions. He had appealed to the State Social Welfare Board without success and he had made the rounds of every ophthalmologist in town. He was a frequent caller at our office and was not to be denied the chance to see me, although I had to give him the same answer that everyone else did.

My office was in the rear of the building, and Herb frequently looked in the window to see if I was there. The windows were shaded and curtained, but Herb's sight seemed to penetrate these objects with ease. If I was there he proceeded to the reception desk and asked to see me. On several occasions the receptionist did not know I had returned to the office and told Herb that I was not in. His moment of triumph was when he could contradict her by saying I was in—because he had seen me through my office window.

He appeared at a crowded session of the Board of Supervisors one Tuesday morning, and as he came cautiously down the aisle with his cane exploring the benches on each side a handmade sign dangled from his neck and stated, in crude but bold lettering, THE WELFARE DIRECTOR IS STARVING ME! The board members were just a little bit upset and I got a call to hurry down and get Herb out of the board room. We rode back to the office and once again discussed the reasons why he could not get on welfare. Herb was persistent but he held no grudge. The board room appearance was in his opinion a good try, and he was disappointed that it failed, but he seemed to hold no hard feelings and I wondered what and where his next attempt would be.

Herb's Good Shepherd must have been in attendance at the next meeting of the State Social Welfare Board, for it adopted a new regulation which was the answer to his prayers. The regulation provided for those who were physically sighted but psychiatrically blind. This was a concession to those who were not blind but would not see, and Herb fitted this category to perfection. He convinced a psychiatrist that he thought he was blind and became eligible for aid.

Having achieved his objective, Herb became mellow, apologized for yelling at the girls in the office and invited me out to his home to see him. The next few months were featured by pleasant telephone calls from him and renewed invitations. The pressure of work kept me in the office and I did not get to visit Herb. One foggy morning, about a year after he had received his first check, his wife called to tell me that Herb had passed away and to give me a last message. He had left instructions that I be reassured that we were friends and that he appreciated all the help we had given him. I was saddened and regretted that the demands of daily working and living had kept me from visiting him. I liked Herb; he was a worthy opponent. He had an objective and he achieved it. If Saint Peter has a welfare program on the other side, Herb will be on it, regardless of the requirements.

Erwin stood straight but he said he had a low back pain and no one could disprove it. He was, when he chose to work, an excellent auto mechanic. Two things, however, stood in his way: his wife, in spite of his bad back, continued to produce a larger and larger brood of children, and he liked to gamble. As the gap narrowed between his income and that required for basic maintenance of the household, he had less for the Chinese lottery and the card games in the rear of the pool hall. He saw welfare as a solution to his problem and made application.

It was not too difficult for him to convince a doctor that he was in bad shape, and his application was approved. His welfare check did not allow much for gambling and he began to work part of the time. He neglected to report his earnings and was doing quite well. He now had more time to gamble and he had a little more money to do it with. All went well until some neighbor, who was tired of the rise-and-shine routine, made a complaint to the welfare department. The investigation which followed resulted in a conviction for fraud, and Erwin was admonished by the court and told not to do it again.

He returned to full-time work for awhile but soon tired of the routine, particularly that which kept him from his favorite haunts. He applied again and was accepted. He worked part time and gambled part time and failed to report his earnings. The complaint, investigation and courtroom procedures were repeated and he returned to work. It would be well if this were the end of the story and the end of Erwin' jousts with the welfare department, but they were repeated many times. He always found work, located a sympathetic doctor, applied for welfare and later confronted a kindly judge.

The last time I saw Erwin he still stood straight and tall, and he had been on welfare for some time. My guess is that he is still following the old routine and that either he has been better able to conceal his activities or that his intolerant neighbor has died from overwork.

There is an adage among people who work in welfare departments that anyone who tries long enough and hard enough can get on welfare. Erwin proved this theory to the hilt. Welfare was the answer to his problem and for him a way to work a little, gamble a lot and to continue to spawn children.

Incapacity is an interesting subject and one about which there are opposing opinions. Our definition of incapacity for purposes of welfare assistance has become much more broad and liberal than it used to be. There are, however, those among us who maintain that there is no such a thing as incapacity but that there are varying degrees of the will to work. Ike and his wife would seem to give support to this view. Ike came to the welfare department with a diagnosis of Berger's disease, an affliction which is supposed to be both incapacitating and terminal. He had already lost some fingers and, according to the medical diagnosis, would lose other extremities before death overtook him. His wife had internal cancer which was also diagnosed as terminal. It was not difficult to qualify both of them for Aid to the Disabled, and the outlook was for a few months of assistance before the Grim Reaper took them from the welfare rolls.

Two months after their initial application, Ike came to the department with a startling report. He did not know about the fifth amendment, but his wife was romancing with a neighbor, and even if he had been informed, his anger would have overridden his fears of self-incrimination. A neighbor who was affluent was supporting Ike's wife in a manner to which she was completely unaccustomed, and not only was his wife romantically involved with the neighbor but Ike of the terminal affliction was working and had been steadily employed for a year and a half. The report on his wife's activities and his unreported income made them subject to arrest for fraud. This was one case, however, where the district attorney did not press for a complaint. It would be difficult to imagine either a judge or a jury meting out punishment to two people living on borrowed time.

There are many welfare recipients who make determined efforts to get off the welfare rolls, and there are those who accept welfare on an as-needed basis.

Chin Lo is an elderly, dignified Oriental gentleman of some eighty-two years. He came in to the office recently to bow low and to anounce ceremoniously that he was going to the fields to work and would see us again next fall when the crops were in. We gauge the seasons by Chin's applications for aid and his requests for discontinuance. His November appearances mean that the harvest is over, the rains are on the way and winter is near. His polite goodbyes in March herald the coming of spring, the certainty that most of the danger from frost is over and that crops are being planted again. Work is strictly a voluntary act on Chin's part. He is old enough and has such few possessions that he could coast through the rest of his days as the recipient of an old-age pension.

Someday I expect that Chin Lo will be found at the end of a long crop row and that he will be in that everlasting slumber which comes, as it must, to all of us. With Chin's slumber will end a tradition of industry and habit which are a rare commodity in a person of his years. I have been expecting his demise for many years, however, and Chin Lo and his traditional visits are still with us.

The "rugged individualist" unfortunately became a political phrase during the launching of Roosevelt's New Deal, and its political connotation has concealed the fact that such individuals actually still exist. Everybody was worried about Rex the hermit except Rex himself. He had been a wanderer for most of the adult years of his life. He had followed the grain thrasher through the harvests of the great Midwest. Later he had emigrated to California and had become a fruit tramp. The lure of gold and the hope of striking it rich in the mountains brought him to the edge of a river which had its origins in the eternal snows of the back country. Here on a sandbar which had once been a part of the river bed, Rex constructed a shack and panned the stream for flashes of the precious metal. As time went on, gold became more and more scarce and its price through government decree remained at a fixed level.

Fortunately he was a neighbor to those whom we have delegated responsibility for upkeep and guardianship of our great forests. There seems to be something about working with nature which brings not only an understanding of the mysteries of life but a compassion for one's fellow man. Forest rangers had watched over Rex for several years and had helped him to the extent his independence would permit. They were engaged in building trails through the mountains and asked Rex to come to work for them. He proved to be somewhat less than a placid employee. His years alone by the roaring river plus his advancing age had convinced him that there were evil spirits about and that they were out to get him. As he shovelled dirt and dug rocks out of the root-tangled earth, small rock slides triggered by gravity or earth tremors would send pebbles and boulders bouncing near him, and an occasional one would score a direct hit. With the rocks were mingled the "voices of the spirits," and Rex replied in kind by cursing the "spirits" and hurling rocks at them.

The compassion of the Forest Service was finally strained, and one of the rangers called to see what welfare could do for Rex. We were cautioned to send multiple members of the male sex to see him and to prepare them for an unusual reception and a possible hostile reaction. The caseworkers found him working on a trail and engaging in a debate and rock-throwing contest with the devil. He did not know what welfare was and did not want to find out. He did want some help with the evil spirits, but this kind of activity is, unfortunately, not recognized by the Federal government as a reimbursable welfare "service."

Rex is still working for the Forest Service. The rangers will take good care of him until the spirits make their final call at his cabin. The chances are that they will be good spirits and Rex will be able to construct trails in the Great Beyond without interference from rock-throwing demons. If this kind of labor is not available, he will be doing something else. It is a sure thing that he will not be asking how he can get on welfare.

Charlie wanted to get off the "pension." While welfare assists millions of persons and is a recognized obligation of government, it still has some stigma attached to it, particularly in the minds of the elderly who are of a generation which measured a man by his capacity for physical labor. Charlie's attempts at getting off pension rolls were persistent but not practical. He entered every puzzle contest which came along, expected always to win, and always lost.

I first become acquainted with Charlie when a gravelly voice on the telephone invited me to meet him under an elm tree at a specified location. I accepted with some reservations and began a relationship which was to continue for several years and which consisted almost entirely of listening on one end of a telephone line while Charlie talked on and on.

I will always believe that he possessed an unusual degree of extrasensory perception. There were months on end when the beginning of our evening meal coincided to the second with a telephone call from Charlie. If we ate early, he called early; if dinner was late, Charlie was on the phone just as I sat down at the table.

He usually opened the conversation by recounting his latest efforts at financial independence and his assurance that next time he was going to make it. In his early years he had been a salesman and had travelled over the countryside by horse and buggy. He had a host of friends and acquaintances and would recount personal experiences with the famous names of bygone years.

There was no opportunity for rebuttal with Charlie; when he called, I listened and I stopped listening only when he was ready to quit talking. I have signed documents authorizing the expenditure of millions of dollars while Charlie recounted tales of being stranded in rural locations and spending nights in barns, sheds or other appurtenances. Incurring the displeasure of my family, I have eaten dinner with the phone to my ear and Charlie's voice crackling over the line. Saturdays, Sundays and holidays were no exception, for Charlie's urge to talk knew neither calendar nor season.

One night, Charlie's voice, which at best sounded like it was being strained through coarse gravel, was hesitant and his words were jumbled. He said he thought he had suffered a stroke. He had done nothing about it and had not called a doctor. The medical profession in general constituted his most deeply rooted dislike, and it took me a long time to convince him that I should bring a doctor to see him. He would permit this intrusion into his prejudice only on my promise that the doctor I would bring was a "right guy." Our departmental medical consultant was a skilled general practitioner with many years of experience, but even he was not quite prepared for Charlie and his theories on medical care. It took a period of gentle persuasion before Charlie consented to shed his shirt and allow the doctor to make an examination. As his undershirt slid off his bony superstructure a metal object was visible on his abdomen. It proved to be a fruit jar lid whose pierced edges were threaded with string. The string was tied at his back, keeping the fruit jar lid firmly in place over a hernia which Charlie stated he had acquired many years before. Medical education had not prepared the good doctor for this innovation, and he was so amused that Charlie's physical examination proceeded with some difficulty.

There was no doubt that Charlie had suffered a slight stroke. The doctor prescribed rest and some medication, and we prepared to leave, but Charlie was not to be denied the opportunity of talking to a captive medical audience and he proceeded to give us his pitch for a "cancer cure." When it came to the specifics he was very indefinite. He usually mentioned honey and iron and a salve which he claimed to have mixed himself. He cited numerous "cures" and much opposition by doctors, which was apparently the basis of his feeling towards them. He did not plan to make any profit from his remedy, but after winning a puzzle contest he intended to travel far and wide and distribute his "cancer cure" to the afflicted.

Charlie was old and ill and I think the puzzle contests and the "cancer cure" were all that kept him alive and talking. Late one night a neighbor heard his radio playing very loudly, and the next morning she and the landlord found Charlie dead on the bathroom floor of his apartment. With all his plans for accumulating money, he died with less than enough to pay for a modest funeral, and he had no burial plot. A local funeral director who knew him provided a service and burial arrangements, and a local lodge, to which he did not belong, gave him a burial plot in a private cemetery.

There were only three of us at the funeral services. A couple who lived next door to Charlie shared a bench with me in a large and otherwise empty funeral chapel. During the services I thought of a promise I had given Charlie and the fact that I could not keep it. He had willed me his "cancer cure" and had made me promise to promote its distribution. The difficulty of carrying out this charge was that Charlie had been so secretive about the "cure" that he had never revealed its formula to me.

How can you get on welfare? You can if you try long and hard enough and if you reduce yourself to circumstances which are on the margin of a financially precarious position. Why would anyone want to get on welfare? Why do some of us envy those for whom welfare is the only answer to the pressing problems of food, clothing and shelter? The answers to these questions may be evident to some but they are unknown to those of us who work and dwell in the welfare world.

A colleague of mine becomes particularly upset when an affluent person inquires about getting on welfare. The last time I saw him he was threatening to resign from the human race. Maybe this is one answer to the inevitable question.

Chapter III

Thrice-told Tales

O<small>N OCCASION</small>, workers in our department inform my secretary that they have exhausted all their efforts in attempting to explain why someone can not have what he wants and that the disappointed person wants to see me. I do not recall having refused to see anyone, although I face each situation with mixed emotions. The social worker and his supervisor have usually given a good and legal reason why we cannot do something, and I am bound by the same laws they are. I am usually somewhat apprehensive, for invariably the person coming to see me is larger than I am and is always angry, and there is no rear exit from my office.

Jim had been off and on aid for more than six years. He was a stepfather to four dependent children and we had had a most difficult time with him. There were numerous occasions when he had failed to apply for a position to which he had been referred. The worker told me that this was the same old story: he had been referred to a job at a local manufacturing plant and had failed to file an application. His face was very flushed when he entered the room and he was visibly upset and angry. He had some difficulty expressing himself and I explained the necessity of his accepting employment when it was available.

He jumped to his feet and started pacing the room, and I had visions of involuntarily leaving the building through the third-story window. With a visible exertion he said, "Do you want to know what's wrong with me?" When I answered in the affirmative he raised his voice to a high pitch and poured out a torrent of words. "I can't read or write," he said. "I've been here for six years and couldn't tell anybody about it because I was ashamed.

27

I'm not lazy and I want to work, but when one of your workers sends me out on a job and they push an application through the window, I'm dead." He seemed greatly relieved to have gotten this long-time burden off his chest, and as we discussed his enrollment in a literacy class he seemed to sense a new purpose in life.

We had thought he was lazy. Many people think that all welfare recipients are lazy; actually, few of them are. They represent a cross section of life, but they do have one common general characteristic, and it is not laziness, race, dishonesty, or a general attitude of dependence. Jim was expressing the most common characteristic by revealing that he lacked formal schooling. In general, welfare recipients lack adequate formal education and are untrained. They are ill equipped to compete in a world which demands technology and skills. High-school graduates among them are a small minority and are quite frequently outnumbered by those on the other end of the scale who are unable to read or write. One of our greatest failures in the field of prevention of dependence is the young school dropout who today "drags the main" in his souped-up hot rod but who tomorrow will be filling out an application in a welfare office.

If Hans Christian Anderson were alive today, he would have to extend his imagination to equal the fantastic tales about welfare which are circulated far and wide. They are so repetitive in substance that they reach the point of monotony. In fact, we do not get much time to explain what welfare is because we are forced to spend so much time telling people what it is not.

Every year when the county adopts its budget for the fiscal year there arises a familiar cry. Welfare is declared to be more than half of the county budget. Rather wearily the welfare department explains that the welfare budget is 84 per cent state and Federal money, that the total property tax bill is more than seventy million dollars and that the welfare property tax bill is less than seven million dollars. We patiently explain that the so-called county budget is only about 20 per cent of the total property tax funds spent each year and that schools, cities and special districts spend the largest part of the local property tax dollar. All of this is to no avail; people have read the headlines in the local paper and we might as well save our breath. Next year the newspaper will once again announce that the welfare budget is more than half of the county budget and the show will start all over again.

In any given community, most of its citizens have never had occasion to visit the local welfare office. This, however, in no way limits their imagination as to what occurs there. The average citizen has visions of a dodge-gate type of operation where people make free and unfettered choices. One side of the gate leads to a window where money is passed out in generous quantities with no questions asked. The other side leads to work and, of course, this is a very thin line.

A frequent critic of welfare called our office recently to complain that he needed employees and to state that he wished we would not encourage people to refuse work offers. I told him that our waiting room was filled and that if he would come to the office he could have his choice of anyone in the waiting room as a prospective employee. He came and after muscling his way through the line at the reception window stayed only long enough to assure himself that there were no employable people available. He stated that he would not employ anyone he saw and that he did not think anyone else would either. He concluded on what was a rather mellow note for him by saying that there were many unfortunate people and that he guessed they had to be cared for someway or another.

One of the most consistent beliefs about welfare is that women conceive children in order to qualify for extra welfare benefits. Unfortunately the opposite is true. The majority of women who have illegitimate children and who receive welfare do not want the children who are the products of their extramarital adventures.

Mary is a typical example in some ways. She is more promiscuous than most and is certainly less careful about exercising any degree of birth control or family planning. She has had eight children by as many different fathers and is still of child-bearing age. While she has ready access to birth control advice and supplies without cost, she will not be bothered with this responsibility. Her children are reared on the thin edge of neglect. They do have a fairly adequate supply of the physical necessities of life, but they were unwanted before birth and are unwanted now, and they know it. They lack love, the ingredient most necessary to produce well-adjusted, normal children. They will be problems for schools, police, health departments, neighbors and society in general. The chances are that they will wind up on the welfare rolls in future years. Mary may not know all this but welfare does. It is a dreary cycle of real-life drama that we have seen many times over.

It is most unlikely that Mary had dollar signs in her eyes at the times conception occurred. It is more likely that she felt like the man who had a large family and was advised to do something at the climax of the act of procreation and who replied that at such times he felt like he could support the birth of a nation. Mary and her colleagues are careless, lonely, easily taken in, sometimes amoral and occasionally immoral. They are not economy minded, for if they were, the few extra dollars of welfare added for each additional child would be no inducement to enter into clandestine affairs.

The mother of an illegitimate child in our society bears the burden of her guilt, the inconvenience of pregnancy and some measure of responsibility for care and supervision. The father usually goes scot-free and blithely sows his plentiful seed in other fertile beds. The real victim, however, is the child, who even in this enlightened age has three strikes against him before he ever gets up to the plate. His biggest handicap is that he is unwanted, and as an unwanted child he has a better than average chance of growing up to join the ranks of the hostile rebels who exhibit psychopathic behavior, become behavior problems, sex deviates and cop killers. With all the inherent problems in illegitimacy, society would be much better off if the fable were true that the mother deliberately conceived the child for economic gain. Under those circumstances he would be given some reason for being.

Welfare recipients, like many taxpayers, sometimes think the caseworker and the welfare director are all-powerful and that they make the rules up as they go along. A frequent complaint is to the effect that "my worker is mad at me," or "my worker doesn't like me." If their grant is reduced they think the caseworker assigned to them did it for spite and that if they could only get to someone "higher up" all their problems would be solved. They seem to envision workers and welfare directors who work entirely on whim.

Under this belief, if the day starts out on a negative note for either the director or caseworker, all welfare checks will be reduced that day.

There is no other function of government which is as rigidly controlled by law and regulation as is public welfare. The welfare departments operate out of a series of state and Federal "bibles" which are explicit to the penny. While some state officials complain bitterly about the "Federal yoke," they eagerly accept the Federal money which pays for more than half of welfare costs. The old story about not having one's cake and eating it at the same time is particularly apropos of welfare. One accepts money from the Federal and state governments and does what they say. The demands of local governmental officials for local discretion in welfare spending will continue to be ignored as long as Federal and state governments are paying most of the bill.

We have a local radio station which features a call-in program. Some of the statements which are made are far removed from the realm of responsibility. I understand that some of our citizens have been quite upset and have complained to the Federal Communications Commission, but the program is a popular one and evidently provides a medium for some people to get things off their chest even if they are repeating some far-fetched story which has no basis in fact. I tuned into this program recently to hear that welfare workers from our department were canvassing the county, knocking on doors and announcing that they do not have enough to do and requesting that people apply for welfare. The story gets better as it goes along by announcing that our employees are paid on some kind of piecework basis and that the more cases they carry, the greater salary they receive.

I really wish the spinner of this yarn could be assigned 350 cases in one of the more difficult districts and, after a trial at this, that he could listen to the complaints of social work staff about high caseloads. The complaints are very frequently justified, with recipients demanding services and additional money at the same time that grocers, landlords, friends and acquaintances are describing her as the root of all welfare evil. The lot of the caseworker in public welfare is no bed of roses. I have asked many things of our employees on occasion, including more production under increased pressure, overtime when they were dead-tired and courteous answers in reply to rudeness and insults. I have never asked them to solicit for more cases—I would not dare! Actually, welfare workers and directors are, as a whole, conservative, middleclass people. I recall one year when I was representing our association at the annual legislative session and asked our staff members for suggestions on changes in existing welfare laws and what they would recommend in the way of new laws. Their suggestions were most drastic, and if they had been enacted they would have resulted in a vastly different program from that which we were administering.

One cold winter night I was scheduled to speak to a farm organization in a small rural town. The schoolhouse where we met was well heated but the attitude of the group towards welfare was more frosty than the weather outside. They complained bitterly about welfare in general and some "cases" in particular. I have made it a habit to take a pad of paper and a pencil with me on such occasions, but when I suggested that some of the complaining members of the audience give me names, addresses and dates, they offered a variety of excuses for not doing so. It was evident that they were repeating some of the oft-told tales about welfare and could not vouch for the circumstances themselves. It was also obvious that they were not talking about welfare in general but only one welfare program—the aid for dependent children. In their approaches to the rumored "case" and the concentration of their criticism on the children's program, they were following a pattern established by other groups at other times and other places.

After I had listened to their complaints for some time I asked them how many of their parents and other elderly relatives were recipients of old-age assistance. A majority raised their hands without any hesitation. When I ventured to state that old-age assistance was also welfare and that it accounted for a large percentage of welfare expenditures, they exhibited signs of shock and disbelief. They accepted aid to aged persons as a "pension"; they did not connect it with welfare and certainly not with what they considered a program to support immoral mothers of illegitimate children.

It is generally agreed among those who know welfare best that people get on welfare for a number of reasons. Some welfare recipients are just not adequate to compete in a modern industrialized society. In the days when the wielder of the pick and shovel was in demand, he had a place in the sun. With mechanization, industrialization and automation he has long since lost it. There are others who have sufficient native ability but who lack formal education and occupational skills. Some are the victims of tragedy and long spells of chronic illness which destroy their capacity to produce and deplete their economic resources. Who among us could withstand a chronic illness of twenty years' duration? There are some few in number whose only difficulty is that they have lived much longer than they anticipated and the estate which would have carried them through a normal span of three score and ten has dwindled away.

A woman from this group came to our office recently to apply for old-age assistance. Her husband had died several years ago and had left her in comfortable financial circumstances. She was now eighty-eight years of age and was still in good physical and mental health. She came from a very prominent family and was chagrined by circumstances which had brought her to the welfare department. She said that she had planned and expected to live until she was seventy-five years of age but that her good health and longevity had dissipated her financial resources. This could happen to others who have planned for an average period of retirement.

Public welfare is unfortunately known by its failures. It cannot reveal its successes without violating the confidence of individuals who might be harmed by disclosure. Those who have been recipients of welfare and who have risen to financial success are loath to reveal their less fortunate past.

There is a public officeholder from the northern section of our state whose aged parents were at one time recipients of old-age security. He had amassed considerable wealth prior to his election to public office but had known some lean years previously. During the time he was less affluent he made contributions to our department for support of his parents as is required by law. As his income increased he contributed more, and as soon as he could he assumed full responsibility for their support. When he came to our office to announce that he would support his parents, he told us that he had been raised on Aid to Needy Children and that without welfare he did not know what he or his family would have done. I would venture to guess that few if any of his colleagues or constituents are aware of his welfare background. He is a very successful man but welfare can take no credit for his achievements without being a source of embarrassment to him.

Rehabilitation is one of those wonderful words like *motherhood* and *virtue*. Everyone is for it and no one is against it. Everybody thinks that all we need to do is to rehabilitate welfare recipients and all these unpopular programs will disappear and the tax rate will return to what it was in the good old days. This would make a beautiful picture and welfare would replace a great deal of its unpopularity with public approval. It is too bad that things cannot be that way. Welfare workers, who have served as whipping boys for all sorts of social and economic troubles, would certainly enjoy a change of status.

More than half of the recipients of welfare are, by no stretch of the imagination, candidates for rehabilitation. Any attempts to retrain and employ an aged woman of seventy-five years, an elderly blind person or a totally and permanently disabled individual would be ridiculous beyond description. With a flooded labor market and a business world where the forty-five-year-old job seeker finds extreme difficulty in obtaining employment, trying to rehabilitate the aged, blind and disabled does not merit any sensible consideration. These, however, constitute the people for whom more than 60 per cent of all welfare expenditures are made. This leaves the parents of dependent children as the sole candidates for the rehabilitation process. They do not as a whole present an optimistic picture as prospects for training and the labor market. Educationally they are overwhelmingly dropouts. Very few of them have any demand skills, and their work experience has generally been of an unskilled and an off-and-on nature. If a welfare director could rehabilitate and return 10 per cent of this group to self-supporting employment every year he would be hailed as an outstanding success. With increasing automation and industrialization the future looks even less promising, while desertion, the greatest factor in placing minor children on welfare, continues at an accelerated rate. *Rehabilitation* is still a wonderful word, but welfare unfortunately has more questions than answers and more problems than solutions.

The great American dream envisions the climb up the ladder of success by individuals who started at the very bottom. The great American daydream is that public welfare and all its problems will disappear some eventful day and that all the lazy bums, the chiselers and the immoral will become productive citizens. This is a nice dream but it really *is* a dream. The signs of the times point to more automation and less unskilled labor. The school dropout rate maintains its pace. We are less and less concerned about the financial plight of our relatives, and while we condemn government in one breath we ask it to assume additional responsibilities with the other. Public welfare itself is so controversial that it may well not survive the next decade. If it does not, it will have to be replaced by something else which will care for those who are unable or unwilling to care for themselves. It is not likely that the millenium will arrive and that all of our problems will disappear. We will be changing our politically elected leaders from time to time, but history and the course of human events have a long-time habit of shaping the path which leaders of the people follow.

People like to talk about the "good old days" and do some wishful speculation about a future without problems. Public welfare is a catchall for problems. It has been with us in some form or other for a long time, and the chances are that it will continue to be the companion of future generations.

Possibly the most that can be hoped for is that the taxpaying public will become a little better informed about welfare. If it becomes informed and realizes that welfare is a creature of law and regulation formulated by elected representatives and that it is not something conjured up by social workers on a day-to-day basis, then the taxpayers may change welfare to fit the pattern they choose, for in the final analysis the public can have any kind of welfare program it wants or none at all. The choice is up to us, but from past experience we will continue to weave fantastic tales about welfare and as we pass them on we will add a little to them until we believe they are true.

Chapter IV

The Irresponsible Relative

IN THE YEARS since 1935, American public welfare has witnessed a spectacular revolution in our cultural attitudes toward aged parents and other relatives. It has viewed the rise of modern suburbia and the motel and the decline of the American family home as it existed at the beginning of the twentieth century. In this comparatively brief period of time the responsibility for financial and physical care of our relatives has shifted from the American home to the American government. Our increase in national affluence has been accompanied by a loss of personal concern for our kin.

The home of my boyhood was not so different from that of my playmates and the other homes surrounding it, but its atmosphere and its daily activities were a far cry from that of our modern American residence. I lived in the lower age group of a large family in a small rural town. Our family life from day to day resembled a grand central hotel being operated by the Salvation Army. There was never a stranger who passed our door without entering and we were always host to a myriad of near and distant relatives, ex-hired hands, friends, or relatives of some distant relation of ours and a gathering of down-and-outers. Our home would never have passed modern requirements for a foster home license, and if we had ever made application to adopt a child from a present-day adoption agency the Child Welfare League of America would have taken the matter to the highest court in the land. We slept two in a bed and on occasion three. There were countless occasions at all hours of the night during my youth when a gentle nudge and a request to move over would provide one of my brothers and me with an additional bed partner. When I awakened the next morning I might be acquainted with our nocturnal intruder, but quite frequently he would turn out to be someone I had never seen before.

Our family kitchen was a large room with a long table which stretched from corner to corner. On one side was a large kitchen range and on the other a large dish cupboard with a counter which we called a sideboard. I cannot recall a time when there were not one or more guests at our table, and quite frequently the number of "guests" made it necessary for the younger set to eat while standing at the sideboard. Our elders always told us that if we stood up to eat we would grow tall, but we had little confidence in this supposed fringe benefit. In between our regular mealtimes there was usually some knight of the road who, with battered hat in hand, politely inquired about the prospects of something to eat. My father always welcomed these itinerant gentlemen, but my mother was less than enthusiastic about the inconvenience of preparing an in-between meal and usually suggested that there was a woodpile in the backyard and an axe nearby with which our guest should become acquainted.

These visitors to our door came in a steady and consistent pattern, and in spite of my mother's reluctance they were never turned away. We used to wonder if they had marked our door with a recognizable sign, but they also appeared at our neighbors' homes and received the same reception. In fact, my mother was a little more insistent on the woodpile routine than some of our neighbors were and it is likely that in this area of rural charity we donated a little less than our fair share.

Our bedrooms were large and unheated, and they provided space for two or more beds. A situation of this sort in modern surburbia would result in a visit and an admonition from the local child-welfare worker. The large bedroom situation provided for a rigid separation of the sexes. There were bedrooms for boys and bedrooms for girls, but age was no guarantee of individual space or privacy. The younger members of the household were the first to retire and on frosty nights had the dubious privilege of warming the bed, or "breaking the ice" as we called it. When an older brother became engaged we looked forward to his marriage.

It was not that we were pushing romance, but his departure from the home brought a number of distinct advantages. If he was the third bed partner there would be more room when he left. This was particularly pleasing to the youngest member of the trio, who by long tradition occupied the middle position. It also meant that he would not be coming in during the early morning hours and putting his ice-cold feet on our warm extremities.

We accepted all of this with a minimum of concern or complaint and would have been more than surprised if anyone had suggested that we were underprivileged or disadvantaged. Our entire community under standards of the Great Society would have been declared a poverty pocket, and our neighborhood would have provided an unparalleled exhibit for social planners and reformers.

In spite of all this, we lived in a state of comparative contentment and we shared with those who were less fortunate. Any relative who was down on his luck had an open invitation to dwell with us. We never knew the length of time he would be with us— it could be for only a few days or it could stretch into weeks or months and sometimes years. The visitor determined his length of stay and no one ever thought of suggesting that he should leave.

It was traditional that grandparents and aged uncles and aunts would move in with us at a time appropriate to their needs and desires. When this time came they moved into the best rooms and occupied the best beds. This resulted in a series of moves and accommodations which left the lowest age group with the least desirable arrangements. We were reared on the philosophy that "whatever you had you shared with those who had less," and my father consistently preached and practiced the doctrine of helping widows and orphans. There were occasions when I was pitching dusty hay in a widow's barn while my pals played baseball in a nearby vacant lot that I resented my father's philosophy.

These times have faded into the distant past. Affluent Americans build bigger houses than their grandparents did, but there is a room for each son or daughter. Visiting relatives stay at the motel, and aged parents draw old-age assistance or spend their last years in nursing homes. Federal and state governments have repealed laws which made sons and daughters responsible for support of their parents, and the Federal government has enacted new ones which prohibit such laws in state welfare statutes.

The distance we have traveled in shifting our relative responsibilities to the government was brought home to me in a forcible fashion shortly after I went to work for a welfare department. Friday afternoons are noted for crises in welfare departments. Employees are weary after a usually hectic week and are anxious to get out of the building and away from it all. If there is such an individual as a professional welfare applicant (more popularly termed a "chiseler" by the general public), he is sure to appear near closing time on Friday afternoon. His story will be complicated, and rather than attempt to unravel it the social worker will frequently send him on his way with a minimum of assistance and postpone a more thorough look until the following Monday.

One Friday afternoon the director of the general hospital called to ask if I could come to the hospital and help him with a problem. As I walked up the brick pathway I saw the hospital director, a middle-aged man and woman, and an elderly woman on the stone steps which led to the hospital entrance. The man and his wife were by no stretch of the imagination professional welfare applicants. In fact they were an affluent couple, very prominent in social activities in our community. I had a speaking acquaintance with them and I had, on frequent occasions, seen their names in the society section of our local newspaper. The elderly woman was in her eighties and was the husband's mother. She was somewhat senile, as some of us who may live to her age will become, and she appeared to be upset and confused.

The hospital director explained that the couple had brought the husband's mother to the hospital and asked that she be admitted. She had been examined by staff physicians who had determined that she was not in need of hospitalization and had suggested that she could be cared for at home or in a rest home. The hour was late and the hospital director suggested that they return on Monday and that at that time a suitable rest home would be located. They rejected the suggestion that the mother could be cared for at home, and they resisted the delay in getting her into a rest home. It was at this point that the director had called me to reassure them that we would find a home for the husband's mother early Monday morning. I attempted to allay their anxieties and told them that I was certain that a suitable place could be located on the following Monday.

When I was through with my explanation of the proposed plan, the woman took her husband by the arm and said, "This woman cannot stay in my house one more night." They walked down the brick pathway without a backward glance, and the hospital director and I took the aged woman to the reception desk in the hospital and had her admitted as a temporary patient.

County institutions for the poor have an interesting history. Most of them have been abandoned in favor of old-age assistance and other aid programs which permit people to remain in homes of their own choosing. Occasionally a vestige remains which has changed down through the years but still offers shelter to someone for whom the county is responsible. Our county convalescent home had been a poor farm, an old folks' home, and finally a convalescent facility operated in conjunction with the county hospital. During part of its long history it had served as a community catchall for those who had no other place to go. In all its history it had been inhabited by those who had no families, those who had deliberately cut themselves off from their families or those whose families had rejected or abandoned them. When the home was finally closed and its inhabitants moved to nursing homes and other privately owned facilities it left a legacy of records which dated back into the previous century. These were inscribed in large black ledger books and were confined to line entries which gave a brief description of the individual and the circumstances under which he or she entered and left the home. At the end of the factual information was a column for remarks, which frequently spelled out the philosophy of the overseer of the home and on occasion the current attitude of society towards some of its more unfortunate members.

The entrance and departure of an eighteen-year-old girl was highlighted by the statement that she was unmarried, pregnant, Mexican and "no good." One independent character had left because he refused to peel potatoes in the basement. It would not be too difficult to surmise that his departure was not altogether voluntary. The number of guests at the home who had been born abroad constituted a majority. One might surmise that the years they entered the facility were those following the great tidal waves of immigrants to this country, but further investigation might have revealed that in leaving the land of their birth they had lost family ties and with illness and old age had turned to local government for food and shelter. Scattered throughout the pages of the somber volumes were indications that some of the aged and the weary had terminated their stay at the home on a final note, "Died in the Home this date."

In the last few months of its existence the management of the home reverted to the welfare department. It was becoming an obsolete institution, and welfare, which is frequently a depository for functions of county government which do not logically fit anywhere, was selected to preside at its demise. Its population was a varied assortment of men, some of whom were convalescing from hospital care, some who were temporary boarders and a few who had been there for some time and had no other place to go.

Myron had been a resident of the home for more than three years. As a more or less "permanent resident" he had acquired a status to be envied by newcomers and late arrivals. He had a "private" room and a radio and was an unofficial assistant in overall operations. I was told that he could not talk and my first few encounters with him gave weight to this story. He was intelligent and pleasant and he understood very well but his replies were confined to nodding or shaking his head.

One morning when the superintendent of the home and I entered the day room he stationed himself directly in my path. His feet were spread apart and his face was crimson. Myron is a husky individual; it was evident that he was under considerable strain and I wondered if I had done something to offend him. In the first words I had ever heard him speak he shouted a boisterous greeting of "Hello, Boss!" From then on, Myron's vocabulary grew with astonishing rapidity and we engaged in daily conversations. I had considerable concern about his future when the home closed and I was relieved when it became necessary for our department to have a messenger. He accepted this job as if he had been born to it and pushed his messenger cart between our offices with a speedy and relentless pace. We have never found a way to slow him down. He accepts the weather for what it is, and while the rest of us are complaining about the heat or the cold he indicates that it is just right and pushes his cart just a little faster to prove it.

If anyone were to describe the perfect employee he would have to include many of Myron's characteristics. He loves his job, he never complains and he thoroughly likes everyone with whom he works. One of his greatest delights is to put his head around the door to my office and inquire if I am "loafing as usual." The mere fact that members of the board of supervisors or the grand jury are in my office does not deter him in the least. Members of the board, who are my bosses, frequently remind me that he is the one employee in the department who really understands his boss. The convalescent home left us records and memories but its finest legacy was Myron. He has found a home in our department and we have found an invaluable employee. If he ever left us we would have to get at least two men in his place. We do not like to think about that, for no one could really replace Myron.

An owner of a nursing home has told me of a situation in which a son contributes money for his mother's care but nothing else. The mother has been in the home for several years and has occupied a private room. She requires considerable care and receives a maximum of medical and nursing attention. The fee for her care is high, but the son pays it regularly and without complaint. The puzzling aspect of his relationship with his mother is that he appears in the front business office of the home on the first day of the month, pays the bill for his mother's care and departs. In all the years that his mother has been in the home he has never gone down the hall to her room to see her. She lies in her bed surrounded with expert attention but alone with her thoughts.

In desperation or as a prod to action, mothers of minor children sometimes threaten to leave their progeny on the doorsteps of welfare offices. These are usually children whose fathers have already rejected and deserted them, and it must further disturb their sense of security. The mothers are frequently applicants for assistance whose request has been denied, or more frequently they are dissatisfied with the amount of aid they receive or the time being consumed in processing their applications. These threats are usually conveyed via the telephone and can sometimes be countered with an application of calm reasoning. On occasion, however, it becomes necessary to remind a mother that as a parent she has the primary responsibility for support and supervision of her children and that the responsibility of the state is secondary. It also becomes necessary to remind some mothers that desertion of a minor child by a parent is a crime which, in the event it occurs, the state may have to recognize by taking official action against her.

It is difficult to understand how a father could desert or a mother could threaten to abandon children who come to the welfare office, for they are some of the most beautiful children in the world. Given the clothing which is the common-day attire of some children of affluent parentage they would grace the society pages of any newspaper and provide the stiffest competition in any beauty contest. The cruel facts are, however, that three fourths of the children on welfare rolls are there because a parent, usually the father, has deserted them. If parents who beget children would support them, the unpopular Aid to Dependent Children program would shrink to a fraction of its present size. The social and emotional effects of desertion on children are immeasurable, but it is a certainty that they contribute to delinquency, crime, and mental and emotional illness. Regardless of the fine job of child-rearing that many mothers accomplish alone, fatherless children are a lonely group. Let any adult male approach them with kindness and interest and they reach out to him for warmth and affection.

There have been occasions when my father image to a welfare child has been a source of temporary embarrassment to me and to the child's mother and a fountain of amusement to my fellow employees and various other onlookers.

The search for the absent father is a continuing quest in welfare departments, and he sometimes appears in unexpected places. We had two workmen employed in our building on one occasion who were efficient and willing and who were having a wonderful time as they worked. Their world crashed down around them when we accidentally learned that they were absent fathers for whom we had been searching.

I stepped into our office waiting room one day to speak to our receptionist. A towheaded girl of about five years of age was seated on her mother's lap across the room. She jumped to the floor and ran across the room yelling "Daddy, Daddy!" in a most enthusiastic voice. She grabbed me around the legs and held on tight. It took both her mother's efforts and mine to get her away. The crowd in the waiting room was very amused and a congregation of employees had gathered at the reception room window to enjoy my plight. I am not certain that I convinced them that I really was not the absent father after all.

A wise and gracious teacher once helped me out of an equally difficult situation by telling a large assemblage of mothers and children that I looked like everybody's daddy. On this occasion I was speaking to an assembly of mothers in a welfare school and was greeted by an eager childish voice which announced for all to hear: "Look Mommy, Daddy!" The search for the absent father is not confined to law enforcement and welfare; the children also look.

Waiting rooms in welfare departments present a variety of scenes of human interest. Not everyone who comes there is a "needy person" in the language of the welfare statutes. Messengers for business firms, relatives and friends of the needy, and the poor themselves constitute a contrast in circumstances and in reasons for being at the entrance to a welfare department. One who has observed welfare waiting rooms over a period of years does not expect to see much in the way of anything new and different.

I usually walk to or through our waiting room once every day. I am sure this would be labeled by most welfare administrators as an unwise habit, some of whom feel rather strongly about any form of contact with welfare applicants and recipients. There are times when it does give rise to problems. If an applicant recognizes you he is apt to intercept your progress through the room and ask that you take his case over. This request is usually coupled with the statement that the caseworker is a nice person but simply does not understand the problems involved. On such occasions I have to reiterate that I do not take applications and that the case-worker is governed by the same laws, rules and regulations that I am. I assure him that his case will be reviewed by a supervisor and that his situation will be governed by the law which applies to it.

In spite of the occasional encounters, I still make regular visits to the waiting room. My rationale for so doing is that I do not ever want to deal completely with figures and other abstract matters and lose sight of the reason for my occupational existence. As I have perused some case histories I have come to the conclusion that the reception desk is a narrow corridor and but for the grace of God I might well be on the other side.

In spite of all this, however, I was not prepared for the scene which I came upon recently. Seated in a chair in our waiting room was an elderly man in a flimsy, half-opened hospital robe. In the chair next to him was an undershirt and shorts. His feet were clean but bare, and there was no visible evidence of shoes or stockings near him. He was confused and distressed and I stopped to tell him that even though the office was not yet open someone would see him immediately. The social worker who interviewed him and arranged for his placement in a rest home learned that he had been released from a hospital at ten o'clock the previous night. He was very vague and uncertain about friends or relatives and could not recall how or where he had spent the night. The chances are that he did have relatives somewhere, but they apparently had not kept in touch with him.

Public assistance and public health care are wonderful services for those who need them, but they are big in scope and structure, and the individual without friends or relatives sometimes gets lost in their mass impersonal approach.

It has been evident for many years that we are not going to return to the old-fashioned philosophy of the personal assumption of responsibility for care of our needy relatives. For better or for worse, depending upon one's age and his philosophy, the good old days are not coming back. We are not going to sleep three in a bed and six in a room and we are not going to open our doors and our checking accounts either to our down-and-out relatives or to the needy strangers who cross our paths. We are quite firmly committed to entrusting the responsibility for such care to our various governmental agencies. In all this, however, we cannot have our cake and eat it too. As long as we do not want to care for our aged parents and other relatives, someone else will have to do it. The ironic part of this situation is that some of our good citizens who complain in the loudest and most bitter fashion about welfare costs are the first and most insistent in reminding the welfare department of its obligation to take care of their relatives.

If we could put the economic issues aside and form a partnership of interest with government in caring for our relatives it would be a much more humane and ideal situation than that which now exists. This is an ideal, however, which those closest to the situation do not expect to see evolve. There are some notable exceptions, but they are in the minority, and by and large we are irresponsible where our unfortunate and needy relatives are concerned.

Chapter V

Grand Juror Mania

T HE GRAND JURY as an institution of government has become almost as controversial as public welfare. A good part of this arises from the vagueness in the law defining the powers and duties of a grand jury and a considerable portion is occasioned by the activities of grand jurors themselves.

An eminent student and practitioner of the legal arts in our community has his own interesting theory. He contends that when nineteen good stable citizens are sworn in as grand jurors, a strange malady attacks them. They become convinced that all government officials are dishonest and corrupt and that the salvation of the county rests upon the shoulders of the grand jurors. Accordingly, they put on their armor of preconceived notions, mount white chargers and ride off to the fray. Local government officials who have had contact with grand jurors will concede that this theory has considerable merit.

Every year, all over the country, grand jurors are selected, the jury is impanelled and instructed, and a study is made of local government. The members of the grand jury are selected from a list of citizens submitted by superior-court judges. There are some individuals who volunteer for service on the grand jury and are eager to serve. In all too many instances those who volunteer have made up their minds about local government before they are selected and they are anxious to get in and "clean up the mess." They sometimes have a particular function of government selected for scrutiny and will ask to serve on the committee which will report on that particular governmental function.

The attitude and accomplishments of the grand jury are largely determined by the instructions they receive from the presiding judge who impanels and instructs the jury. There are judges who have particular ideas about certain functions of local government and will turn the efforts of the grand jury in that direction. Judges in the American court system run from the ridiculous to the sublime, and with our strong respect for the judicial system it is somewhat of a shock to realize that judges are also human and that they have all the prejudices, preconceived notions, and feelings that are common to the general population. Some are not content with the tremendous power which the bench gives them and would like to extend their influence over functions of government with which they are not primarily concerned. Fortunately, most grand jurors are wisely selected, carefully instructed, and operate during their tour of duty within the legal framework which limits the powers of grand juries.

There are, however, grand jurors who seem to have carried over from their younger years an intense desire to see mystery in everything and an urge to play cops and robbers. Every public official who has served any length of time has experienced the misplaced zeal of one or more of these individuals.

Our welfare department has operated a commissary for many years. It is used for cases of emergency assistance while applications for ongoing aid are processed. Critics of our department are always remarking about the people who receive groceries and the Cadillacs which make regular trips to the commissary. When I first came to work I thought for a while that the critics might have some valid reasons for their accusations. On several occasions I saw expensive automobiles, including Cadillacs, drive up to the window, and I had a number of these checked out. They proved to be cars of relatives, friends and neighbors, and I found that my suspicions were groundless. One new Cadillac arrived on a regular weekly schedule, and I learned that it belonged to the former employer of an aged woman who had no means of transportation.

One of our eager grand jurors must have believed the stories about the expensive automobiles because he commissioned himself to find out the direct way. Stationing himself near the commissary he observed a woman loading groceries into her automobile, and when she left he followed her in his own car. The woman sensed she was being followed and when she stopped at her home and saw that her follower was parked across the street and watching her, she called the police. The guardians of the law arrived promptly and arrested the man as he sat in his automobile. He protested vigorously and told them he was a member of the grand jury and was only trying to do his duty. The arresting officers who were familiar with all the best fabrications considered his story a new high in the con artist game and booked him in the local pokey. He called and asked that I come to the jail and identify him as a member of the welfare committee of the grand jury. He was most grateful to see me and was thereafter a most humble and cooperative member of the grand jury.

Welfare departments present particularly frustrating problems to grand juries. The laws and regulations which determine the course of welfare are formulated at state and Federal levels. The grand jury is a creature of local government and is powerless to alter provisions of assistance programs to which it may be opposed. It is interesting to note that grand juries have uniformly been critical of public welfare and that Congress and the state legislatures have consistently ignored their findings. When a grand jury is hostile in its approach to welfare it brings with it all the misconceptions, the misunderstandings and the controversies which are the constant charges of welfare's most bitter critics.

The welfare department can expect an official call from the foreman of the grand jury shortly after the beginning of each calendar year. There are occasions, however, when a particularly suspicious group will peer around the edges of departmental operations and will question individual employees in hallways and outside the building but will not arrange for any formal or official meeting.

An employee came into the office one morning to report that three men were watching our building from across the street. I indicated that I saw nothing unusual or illegal in this, since we were a public agency and anyone could look at us whenever he wanted to. My interest was aroused, however, when I was informed that the watchers had field glasses, and I went to the window and recognized the foreman of our current grand jury and two members of the welfare committee. Later I learned from a

friend who was a member of the jury that the third member of
the welfare committee had been watching the back door and that
the reason for their interest was to determine if any of our employees were late in arriving at work.

One welfare committee from a grand jury of several years ago
did us a financial favor in an unusually gruesome manner. Supervision of the circumstances under which the indigent dead are
buried has been a welfare department responsibility for many
years. Periodically the funeral directors in our community have
requested adjustments in fees for performing this service, and the
board of supervisors has requested a recommendation from the
welfare department. It is predetermined that our recommendation
will be either for no adjustment or a smaller one than that which
the funeral directors have requested. If it were anticipated that
we would recommend the same figure as was being requested, or
a higher one, our opinion would not be solicited. The members of
the grand jury that year were particularly objective in their approach and they asked if we had any problems with which they
could help us. We mentioned as one of our many problems the
requested increase for indigent burials on which we would be
expected to make a recommendation. Two members of the welfare
committee decided to take this problem as their special project
and began visiting funeral parlors. They did not announce their
official identity and they paid particular attention to caskets
marked for burial of indigents and carefully counted the handles
on each one.

In the contract between the county and the funeral directors
there was a rather obscure clause which provided that caskets for
indigents were to have a certain number of handles. Since each
handle added to the cost of the casket, the jurors felt they should
be accounted for. The deceased indigents, I am sure, were not
concerned whether they were conveyed to their final resting
places by the convenience of four or six handles on their coffins,
but the county was and so were the grand jurors. They found no
shortage of handles, but their visits caused a great deal of concern
on the part of the funeral directors. They felt that they were being
investigated for some unknown reason, and they called our office
to determine if we knew anything about it. When we professed

ignorance it only added to their worries, and they became so concerned that they cancelled their request for an increase and saved us the trouble of making the inevitable recommendation.

Some grand jurors consider themselves as "one-year students of local government." Those who approach jury duty in this frame of mind are apt to acquire a liberal education in the governmental arts and are able to establish a foundation for suggesting constructive improvements. I recall one such jury in particular whose members made a thorough and detailed study of welfare. They read law and regulation, interviewed recipients and social workers and carefully examined case histories. They did not by any means agree with all they observed but they did form enlightened opinions and they did advance some excellent suggestions.

The opposite approach to this has been exhibited by grand jurors who had formed opinions before they looked and who were quite determined not to let the facts get in the way of their opinions. One member of a welfare committee wrote a letter to the foreman in which he claimed to have evidence that the welfare department was "importing Negroes from the South and feeding and breeding them so that they could dominate the county." There have been other grand jurors who, in moments of uninformed but righteous indignation, have pointed to the legal granting of aid as "wholesale fraud."

Perhaps these people and the kind of irresponsible statements to which they give vent should be ignored, but there are always some citizens in the general population who are ready and anxious to believe anything about public officials and governmental activities. One local county official has observed that radical and unsupported statements by members of grand juries "stir up every crackpot in the county."

A number of sessions with a particularly difficult grand jury several years ago led to decisions on my part which have been most beneficial. The unsubstantiated statements they made and the resulting unfavorable publicity were difficult to contend with but the end results were quite the opposite.

The telephone is a wonderful instrument but there are times when welfare directors and other public officials doubt the wisdom of its creation. For many years I had received a steady deluge

of telephone calls at my home after working hours and on weekends and holidays. Some of them were from welfare recipients
and applicants and some were from taxpayers and others who
were unhappy with welfare. There was the one on Thanksgiving
Day from an elderly recipient who said that he was cold and asked
that I get an electric blanket and take it to him posthaste. The
mere fact that it was Thanksgiving Day and that I had no way of
obtaining an electric blanket and getting it to him was strictly
beside the point. He was cold and he wanted an electric blanket;
I was the welfare director and therefore should get him one. I
could not convince him of the practical impossibilities and he was
most unhappy.

There have been numerous occasions on a holiday or weekend
when some concerned recipient called to inquire about his or her
welfare check. They were always surprised when I did not know
exactly where their checks were and usually inquired rather criti-
cally, "Well! Aren't you the welfare director?" I had to admit that
I was but that I just could not keep track of each one of the thirty
thousand checks which were issued from our office each month.
I do not recall any real emergencies which involved odd-hour
telephone inquiries by welfare recipients. I am sure that many of
them thought they were victims of genuine emergencies, but even
if this had been the case there was little or nothing I could have
done about it.

In the course of events I have received telephone calls at very
unusual hours from those who frequent bars and who, having
overestimated their capacities, have acquired an unusual amount
of courage and a desire to complain about welfare. Some of these
calls have been of an abusive and threatening nature. My years
of experience with offenders in the correctional field have convinced me that the man who tells you that he is going to commit
violence is usually the least likely to do so. It is not so easy to convince your young son of this, however, when he reaches the phone
before you do at three A.M. and is told by some drunk that he is
coming your way with a shotgun. I had a series of calls of this
nature in which I could always hear the tinkle of glasses and a
volume of ribald laughter in the background. In a particularly
drunken state one night the caller inadvertently told me his name

and the location of his favorite bar. When law enforcement officers called on him the next day they learned that he was an absent father who objected to supporting his children, and thereafter I heard no more from him.

There are some telephone calls which are not related to the controversial nature of welfare and which do not come from applicants or recipients. These originate with those who view public officials as *public servants* in the literal meaning of the term. The hour or day is of little consequence to them and sometimes they use the stockworn phrase which expresses their sorrow about bothering you at home, and sometimes they do not. One morning at half past six a bright young female voice asked if I could tell her all about welfare. She identified herself as a college student and said that she was writing a term paper. I had just risen and was a little surprised at the timing of the call but told her that I would be glad to see her at the office and would help her all I could. She was unable to conceal her impatience as she informed me that the paper was due at eleven o'clock that morning and that she had to know all about welfare right now!

Members of my staff had urged me for years to get an unlisted telephone, but I felt strongly about serving the public and continued to tolerate the late hour and offbeat calls. It was not until after a number of jousts with a hypercritical grand jury and the resulting rash of telephone calls sprinkled with abuse and threats that I decided to become a little less available. My family and I have since been able to retire at night with some degree of reasonable assurance that we will not be aroused from slumber by someone who has had one too many at the corner bar.

I had developed some unusual working habits over the years and was fast approaching the stage where I was making my wife a welfare widow and my children public assistance orphans. There was never a Saturday, Sunday or holiday when I did not spend a good portion of the day in the office. I attempted to have everything in perfect order for the regular office days which followed. It was only after completely failing to convince some grand jurors of the facts of law and life and after absorbing unusual amounts of criticism and personal abuse that I decided to change my working habits. I still put in the necessary amount of time to get the job done, but I no longer strive for perfection. I reached the conclusion that there was little point in extra effort when the uninformed had all the answers and a lot of the general public was prone to believe them. I have seriously thought of thanking the grand jurors who were responsible for changing my ways, but on second thought I realized they had never believed or understood anything I said, and there was no reason to believe they would react in any different manner to an expression of appreciation.

There are times when it becomes necessary for a harassed welfare director to fight back with unorthodox methods. One grand jury had among its members two corporate farmers whose acreage was counted in sections of land and whose wealth was in seven-figure brackets. They were very critical of public welfare in general and the use of Federal funds by local government in particular. They talked of creeping socialism and the Federal yoke. In the course of discussion with them at a general session of the grand jury, I asked them if they made any differentiation as to how Federal funds were used on the local level. They stated very emphatically that they were opposed to the use of Federal money in any shape or form because it brought domination by the Federal government and corrupted those who accepted it.

I had prepared for this moment for more than a month. It had occurred to me that the two large farmers might possibly be recipients of Federal funds through farm subsidies. The amounts and beneficiaries of farm subsidies is public information, and, while it is not generally published, it is available on request. When I looked at farm subsidies granted in our county, the names of the two grand jurors led all the rest. I casually mentioned that I had information on the subsidy program in our county and I remarked that two members of the jury had each received sizeable amounts. I noted that each member had received an amount considerably in excess of the county's contribution to some of the welfare programs and that I failed to see any difference between a Federal crop subsidy to a farmer and a welfare grant to a needy family. There was an embarrassing silence, but from the nodding of heads it was evident that the nonfarm members of the grand jury were in amused agreement. One of the subsidy recipients finally said that in his opinion there was one big difference. The Federal grant of something for nothing would "corrupt" the welfare recipient, but it would not have the same effect on the big corporate farmer. Needless to say, the matter of Federal funds received no further attention during the remainder of my discussions with that particular grand jury.

I have often wondered why some people want to serve on grand juries. It is a time-consuming task, particularly for those who are busy. In addition, the open-minded citizen who serves must be frustrated when confronted with the mass of laws, rules, regulations, and procedures which are the hallmark of modern American government. I presume that all of us on occasion wonder why the other person chooses to follow his given occupation or why he volunteers for duty on a grand jury. There have also been grand jurors who were curious about the motivations which prompted welfare directors to choose that particular profession. At the end of a long period of questions and answers in a formal meeting of a grand jury, one of its members requested and was granted permission for one more question. He looked at me with evident curiosity and said, "Why do you want this damned job?" I was just a bit startled and did not have an immediate answer, but after thinking a minute I told him that there were two reasons: I had some of the finest people in the world working for me, and although there were disadvantages to the job, the advantages outweighed them. I reminded him as I have often reminded myself that I had the privilege of resigning any time I wished and that no one was forcing me to remain on the job.

The effective future of the grand jury is most uncertain. There have been some judges and individual jury members who tried to extend the activities and powers of the grand jury beyond its prescribed role. There is general agreement among students of the law, however, that the powers of the grand jury are limited to criminal activities and dishonesty in government. Attempts by grand juries to become involved in administrative matters, including personnel management, have been ridiculous exhibitions of uninformed meddling. Their condemnations of Federal and state welfare laws have been fruitless and have been uniformly ignored by legislators and congressmen.

The privilege of serving on a grand jury presents the citizen with an opportunity to study his local government from an advantageous position. It is an institution almost as old as government itself and has a most necessary function to perform. If its members as they are sworn in could somehow be inoculated against grand juror mania, and if they could lose the vision of the knight in shining armor astride the white steed, grand juries could continue to perform useful services to local government and its citizenry.

The chances are, however, that history will continue to repeat itself and that grand juries as functioning bodies will be both ridiculous and sublime. Some will approach their duties with honesty and objectivity, and others will have personal axes to grind. Some will see themselves as the saviors of local government, and others will view a seat on the grand jury as a way station on the road to political careers.

The people who get on welfare will not have to worry much about all of this, but welfare directors will have to continue to contend with grand jurors and will age a bit in the process.

Chapter VI

Author Anonymous

A RANDOM SAMPLING of the daily mail and telephone calls coming to a welfare department would contain such subject matter as to strain the most fruitful imagination. Most of the calls and letters are complaints of one kind or another which, taken together, portray a panorama of anger, frustration, loneliness, illness and sometimes just plain contentious personalities. A number of the letters are unsigned and many of the callers refuse to identify themselves. One's natural inclination is to ignore the anonymous letter and to refuse to talk to the person who does not identify himself. It is difficult to conjure up much respect for the person who wants to complain but refuses to stand up and be counted.

Anonymous complaints run from the very accurate to those which are totally false and are initiated by jealousy, hatred, envy and other negative human emotions. As public agencies, most welfare departments accept and investigate anonymous complaints, including both the verbal and the written ones.

One morning's mail in our office included a postcard which said that a certain absent father was now back home. We had some previous indication that the errant husband had returned, and the social worker had asked the wife about this on a number of occasions. She denied having seen her husband for more than two years or even knowing where he was. After receiving the postcard we decided to look a little closer and assigned the case to the investigators for a morning call. They were admitted to the house, were shown through it, and found no evidence of any adult male living there. They returned to tell me that the complaint was apparently of the "crackpot" variety and we considered the matter closed.

A few days later the mail contained another postcard in the same handwriting as the previous one. It informed us that if we really wanted to find the absent father we should look in the attic and that we would find his clothing under the mattress on the double bed.

On a cold winter morning at about seven A.M. our investigators made another call at the home. They were again admitted, assured that the father was not there, and invited to look through the house. The smaller of the investigators was boosted through the crawl hole in the ceiling. In a far corner of the attic his flashlight revealed the absent father, lying across the joists and without benefit of clothing. He was brought down into the room and an investigator found his wearing apparel under the mattress on the double bed. We never determined the source of the complaint but it had all the earmarks of the so-called inside job. There may have been someone in the family who was not happy to have the absent father return, or it may have been that his wife had found other interests while he was away and that either she or her suitor made the complaint. It would be interesting to know the real story.

On another occasion we had received several verbal complaints alleging that Joe, another absent father, had returned. Joe's wife consistently told the social worker that she had not seen him for several years. Since the complaints continued, however, we again turned to the investigators. They were admitted to the house during the evening hours and were assured that Joe was not there. One of the investigators noticed a pair of large shoes protruding from under a bed at an unusual angle. He reached down and pulled on one of the shoes, and Joe came along with it.

The rejected suitor is a frequent source of anonymous complaints. When his advances are rebuffed he retaliates by informing the welfare department that things are not just what they should be in the home of his would-be girl friend. He expected to make a conquest and is usually bitter about his lack of success.

One such rejected Don Juan wrote an unsigned note stating that our recipient had a lot of money, a new car, and that she was neglecting her children. Our investigation proved that quite the contrary situation existed. The woman had no money, occasionally had the use of her father's car, and was making an excellent home for her children. She readily identified the informer and related how he had called on her, displayed amorous intentions, and was bodily pushed out the back door.

The truism that "hell hath no fury like a woman scorned" results in a rather steady flow of complaints which are anonymous in nature but whose originator can be easily determined because the errant suitor or husband is identified. These are situations where the male of the household has found a greener pasture in the home of a female welfare recipient. The complaints, strangely enough, do not condemn the straying man but picture the woman as a conniving Jezebel who, since she is on welfare, should not be doing that sort of thing. There is little that can be done about these triangles. Welfare law is quite lenient in its view of the roaming male. Many women have told me that the welfare statutes were conceived by men, and they probably were, since they recognize the common-law relationship for welfare purposes. We must consider the present situation in which the sought-after male is found and not the circumstances at the nest he formerly shared with the complainant.

God may help the working girl, but she frequently wonders why welfare does not. She has strong feelings about the member of her sex who is helped by welfare and sometimes gives vent to her feelings via the anonymous communication. The working girl who does not receive welfare is by no means a staunch supporter of public assistance. Like most women, she would prefer to be home with her family. She does not exactly covet the status of a welfare recipient but resents the situation in which she finds herself while others are staying at home. Letters from working girls, even when they are signed, are difficult to answer. The welfare rules and regulations, which require some mothers to work while others do not, are complicated, difficult to explain and quite frequently devoid of logic. The most direct and probably the most accurate explanation would be that in the final analysis those who do not want to work stay at home; it is mostly a matter of motivation. This, however, is far from a satisfactory answer to the woman who resents the necessity of making a living and who sees others in situations which she envies.

There are some complaints about conditions which are hard to believe exist, even though one has experienced and witnessed the unusual. The majority of these turn out to be quite accurate, possibly because they have been observed over a long period of time by neighbors or relatives who have sought help from other sources and have, in final desperation, turned to the welfare department. One of these, which came over my desk recently, stated that an elderly couple receiving old-age assistance were living in filthy surroundings, were alcoholic, and had twenty-four dogs. The writer of this letter must have been an animal lover, for he or she said that the man and woman were probably beyond help but that the writer was concerned about the dogs. This sounded so far-fetched that I debated the idea of having a social worker call but finally decided to do so. The report of the social worker stated that there were indeed twenty-four dogs in and around the house and that the premises were far too filthy to house any healthy canine. The man and woman were both drunk when the call was made and the case record indicated that they had been intoxicated most of the time for several years. The record also related many attempts at helping them, including alcoholic "cures" and periods of time in rest homes and convalescent hospitals. The health department had attempted to get the place in some semblance of a sanitary state but their efforts were also futile. While mismanagement problems are supposed to be characteristic of mothers of dependent children only, this aged couple owed thousands of dollars to local merchants who continued to extend credit to them. This was a situation which appears to be beyond the resources of the community to correct, and the dogs, the filth and the alcohol will continue to be the way of life during the years which remain for this aged couple.

Not all the unpleasant communications to welfare departments originate with recipients and would-be recipients of aid. I have been on the receiving end of occasional calls and letters from professional men which were not professional either in tone or choice of words. The greater portion of these have been where money was involved. There are professional people who can be most unprofessional where finances are concerned. The morning after a national election, one of our community's professional men called and startled me by saying, "Now that you Socialists have put your party in power, when are you going to start paying me?"

Although most polls had predicted the results of the election, I was surprised at the tremendous majorities compiled by some candidates and I wondered if they would interpret the pluralities as mandates in welfare and other areas. I have never been an enthusiastic partisan as far as politics are concerned and share the philosophy that the best election is a close one, regardless of who wins. Needless to say, I was surprised to be identified with any political party and particularly the one traditionally represented by Norman Thomas.

I told my caller that I was surprised that he would accept any money tainted with socialism but that I would try to see that he got his share of it as soon as possible. I also remarked that I was not in the habit of wearing my political affiliations and philosophies on my sleeve but that I hoped he would be able to prove in court that I was a bona fide follower of Mr. Thomas and his associates. The conversation took a sudden and abrupt turn: my caller began addressing me by my first name and reminding me of our many fine and pleasant associations. My memory was just a bit dim in this respect, but I continued to listen as he said that he hoped I could take a joke and assured me of the excellent job I was doing. He concluded by saying that he did not really need the money but was curious as to how we were getting along in converting to payment of medical bills by data processing equipment.

New philosophies and approaches in treatment of the mentally ill have had an important impact on welfare departments. In many states, mental hospitals are no longer accepting the senile psychotic and other mentally ill persons who are not dangerous to themselves or to others. The policy is to leave these people in the community rather than confine them in expensive custodial institutions. One cannot quarrel with this humane and economical approach to the care of the nondangerous psychotic, but it does pose an additional set of problems to welfare departments. There is sometimes a thin judgment line between those who are dangerous and those who are not, and occasionally a supposedly harmless individual will present a dangerous situation to the community and to the welfare department working with him.

I came across an example of this while reading case records of disabled aid recipients. It demonstrated an extreme degree of professional irresponsibility and concerned a man who had been a patient in a state mental hospital. He had been released to return to his home and was receiving assistance from the welfare department. A psychiatrist who had seen him on a routine office call recorded in his medical history that the man was "dangerous to himself, his family and to the community." An extract from the medical record had come to us as a part of the eligibility determination. The psychiatrist had made no effort to warn the man's family or his neighbors nor had he taken any steps to have the man recommitted to the state hospital. If we had not received this information by chance, we would have been sending an unsuspecting and unprotected social worker to call on this man. In any community where the senile psychotics and others classified as harmless are not confined in mental hospitals, the welfare department will be concerned with a larger number of the mentally ill than the department of mental hygiene will be.

The mentally ill have names, addresses and identities, but they dwell in an anonymous world devoid of reality. Their communications with welfare departments are frequently interwoven with fantasy, and their demands can be unreasonable and unrealistic. As one listens to them and reads their letters he is struck by the fact that once they were realistic functioning beings and that the communication is not from the real persons they once were but from an anonymous source unknown to him and to them as well.

A woman who disguised her real identity by a number of assumed titles with religious connotations posed a serious problem for us. She began and ended every sentence with the word "peace," and although this word represents a status of which we could use a lot more in welfare departments, it did not decrease the difficulties involved in attempting to reason with her. She was strikingly beautiful and very persuasive but obviously mentally disturbed. Her story was weird and fantastic, but it may have been true and even today I would not venture a guess. She claimed to be a "spiritual adviser to the poor people" and said that she had $120,000 and a new Cadillac which the "poor people" had given her in return for her spiritual guidance. She had come to our office to seek refuge from an organized crime syndicate which had allegedly chased her out of her home in a southern state and was still pursuing her. She wanted to go to Alaska in order to lose her pursuers and tormenters. The money and the Cadillac were allegedly in a location where she could not get to them without exposing herself to the syndicate and she insisted that we provide her with an airplane ticket to Anchorage. In between persuasive pleas she wept, rolled on the floor and pulled her hair. We could not accept her story and mildly suggested that she might be ill and should seek medical help. She left our office in a hysterical rage, calling down upon us all the curses of the evil spirits. In the brief time she had been in our community she had acquired a considerable following, and the next few days brought a barrage of calls condemning us for our heartless attitude. Shortly thereafter she disappeared and we have not seen her or heard anything about her since.

The disturbed person sometimes turns to God and the Bible for solace and joins with Jehovah and the Scriptures in presenting his point of view and his denunciations of decisions regarding his welfare grant. I was recently informed by mail that God had revealed to an elderly recipient that there were "two pagan traitorous Vipers in the welfare department" and that God, through the Bible, had instructed him that "Ye serpents, ye generation of Vipers, how can ye escape the damnation of hell?" He added that the "vipers" were holding his check because he was a red-blooded American loyal to the "blood-stained Star-Spangled Banner." The letter continued by saying that God had commanded him to write and he closed with a hearty "GOD BLESS YOU." Some unfortunate social worker would have to go to his home and attempt to explain the intricate complications of the Old Age Assistance program to him. If anyone ever needed God's help it would be the worker who had that assignment wished on him.

A very well dressed lady in our community has visited public officials on a regular schedule for a number of years. Some time ago she became a recipient of Aid to the Disabled, based on her mental condition. I had heard many stories about her but had paid little attention to them. Our office is in a large building, and we have a very efficient receptionist, but every so often someone comes in through the employees' entrance and wanders around at will. I looked up from my desk one morning to see a well-dressed middle-aged woman in the doorway to our office. I recognized her as the perpetual visitor to public offices and began to recall, with a degree of apprehension, some of the stories I had heard about her visits. She turned out to be very pleasant and agreeable as she told some startling stories about government officials in our county. According to her, she had been for many years a victim of black magic which had also exerted its powers over certain public officials. She said that there was a tunnel between the courthouse and other county offices which was used to cover up the black magic deeds of county officials. She hastened to assure me that I was a "good guy" and was one who had not been influenced by black magic. I needed much more assurance than this, however, when she opened her purse and revealed a large-caliber revolver which she said was for the special benefit of certain county officials. She left the office, and later I saw her around town on several occasions. I understand that she became a little careless with the revolver and was eventually committed to a state hospital.

Our local newspaper features a column called "Letters From The People," where a wide variety of opinions, complaints and philosophies are printed. Its contents are frequently controversial as is the column itself. Its supporters argue that people should have a right to express their opinions without revealing their identity and that this on many occasions represents the only way the little man can get at big bureaucratic government. Its opponents say that the policy of letting people criticize without signing their names encourages and promotes irresponsibility. Others, who are critical of almost everything our local newspaper does, point out that by choosing which letters will be published, "Letters From The People" actually constitutes a second editorial page for the newspaper where opinions favorable to the policies of the paper can be chosen and printed without anyone's assuming responsibility. They point out that in effect this gives the anonymous letter writer an open invitation to continued irresponsibility.

There is little doubt that a perusal of this section of the paper will reveal a considerable number of irresponsible statements.

There is always a temptation on the part of public officials to answer statements which are not consistent with the facts. This course of action, however, has its drawbacks, since the public official, in order to set the record straight, must use his own name, but the attacker can continue to author false statements under an assumed name or no name at all.

I have followed the advice given to me many years ago by a very astute friend. There had been a series of very inaccurate statements in our local "Letters To The Editor" column and I planned to answer them. My friend pointed out that an accurate answer would not stop the statements and that I should refrain from answering on the basis that "you can't outspray a skunk."

Among welfare's most bitter critics are those who apply for assistance and are denied on the basis of ineligibility. Nothing that happens to them seems right and most of them are convinced that the denial of their application was on a personal rather than a legal basis. Welfare laws permit anyone who wishes to apply to do so, and because of a general lack of understanding of eligibility requirements for the various categories of assistance many individuals apply who are much more affluent that welfare standards permit. This, of course, results in a high rate of denial in some programs, particularly aid to disabled and aid to dependent chilen. Thus, many people come to the welfare department with expectation and leave with feelings of frustration and outright hostility.

A Sunday edition of our local paper carried a particularly bitter denunciation of the welfare department in the "Letters From The People" column. According to the writer, when he visited the welfare department he was treated in a discourteous manner, talked to instead of being listened to and in general had endured a most unsatisfactory experience. I have always been very concerned about the necessity of courtesy and our office has always stressed the point that negative answers which must be given can be delivered in just as courteous a manner as the more acceptable positive replies. For this reason I made a particular effort to identify the writer.

From the address which he gave and the circumstances he described I was able to reconstruct his visit to the welfare department. He was a professional man who was temporarily in financial difficulty and had come to the department to apply for assistance. His basic expectations were that because of his status different rules and regulations would be applied to his situation and different treatment would be accorded him. He saw no reason why the statutory limitations on personal and real property should apply in his case and he attempted to deliver a lecture on how welfare departments in general, and ours in particular, should operate. Unfortunately, the employees in our department, including those who take applications for assistance, are required to work under pressure and on a volume production basis. Although we attempt to be patient and understanding, there simply are not sufficient hours in the day to allow us the privilege of listening to extended philosophical lectures.

One suggestion in the applicant's letter in the newspaper was that employees of the welfare department, including the director, should be required to perform farm labor for a period of time as part of their required training. The rationale for this suggestion was that since farm labor was such hard work and the wages paid were so low, this experience would make welfare employees more sympathetic towards poor people. The suggestion did not really appear to be too practical; a check of the applicant's background revealed that he had never been employed as a farm laborer in any capacity, but more than half of all the employees in the department, including the director, were born and reared on farms. There is an old adage that you can't please a loser, and it would seem that this would apply to our applicant. Had he been granted assistance, his story would have been quite different.

A welfare department does not expect a favorable batting average in any public opinion column and the overwhelming majority of letters about welfare are critical. One day, however, I was more than surprised to see a letter in the daily newspaper which praised our department as the best in the state and even had a few kinds words for me. The glow from this surprising and pleasant experience did not last very long. One week later the men in white got the net around our friend and she began a sojourn in the mental hospital. Some of our employees are convinced that

the basis for her commitment was nothing more than her praise
of our department.

Government-owned vehicles are a convenience and at the same
time a problem for employees who operate them. They carry a
visible identity and other motorists and pedestrians pay particular
attention to them. If a county car is observed going thirty-five
miles an hour in a thirty mile zone, if it is parked at an unusual
angle or if its driver passes a slower vehicle driven by a harried
taxpayer, the department concerned is sure to hear about it. This
does not mean that government vehicles are not used for private
convenience and personal business; everyone knows that this
happens. Those public employees who do occasionally use official
cars for private business would appear to be poor gamblers. They
have a lot at stake for a few cents worth of gasoline. I recall the
case of one state employee who took a state car on a family picnic
to the mountains and was suspended from his job for a period of
six months.

It is reasonable to expect that most departments think they are
watched most closely as far as use of automobiles is concerned.
In our county it seems that the taxpayers assume that all county
cars are operated by welfare personnel. We receive lots of complaints regardless of who is operating the automobiles, but this
may happen to other departments too.

On one occasion we received a written complaint about a
county car which was taken to the home of an employee at night
and parked behind a clump of shrubbery. The car did not happen
to be assigned to one of our employees and we did not pursue
the matter further. A few days later we received another written
communication severely criticizing us for not taking any action.
I learned that the car was assigned to an employee in another
county department, and in the interests of furthering good public
relations for county employees I called the head of the department. When I told him about the report, I expected that he might
thank me but I was impolitely told to take care of my own department and to let other people do the same. Since then I have made
my reports to the county administrative office and have permitted
them to play the role of the good samaritan.

One of the most popular subjects of anonymous letters received in our office produces little or nothing in the way of results. These letters are usually accurate but they contain information which is already known to us. The circumstances they describe are permissible under welfare law, and other than adjusting the amount of money the family receives there is little we can do. These letters tell us that Mrs. Jones has a man living at her house and she is not married to him. In the vast majority of cases we already know about Mrs. Jones' paramour and we have visited the home and informed them of their rights and responsibilities. Our welfare statutes recognize the common-law relationship for welfare purposes. Most people either do not realize this or they refuse to accept the situation on moral grounds, and many of them are shocked and amazed when we tell them about the law. From a welfare director's viewpoint it would appear that our common-law welfare statutes have some similarity to the Volsted Act: the legislators appear to have passed a law to which the majority of citizens are opposed.

I expect that the future will bring little change. Welfare is an unpopular and controversial program, and in all probability it will continue to be everybody's favorite target. People will continue to complain about it, anonymously and otherwise, and we will continue to investigate the complaints. Some of them will be very accurate and some will be ridiculous, but they will continue to constitute an important part of the daily mail.

Chapter VII

Sex In Welfare

THE MODERN LITERARY WORLD has brought discussion of sex to the pages of best sellers. There are more literary efforts which highlight sex than there are those which ignore it. Many people are of the firm opinion that the book without a chapter on sex is doomed to failure. As they peruse they look for a chapter on sex, and if they do not find one they put the book aside for further consideration.

The man on the street and the housewife over the backyard fence have visions of welfare recipients as lustful creatures who while engaging in illicit sexual excursions are busy tabulating the extra benefits which will begin nine months later. One who is well acquainted with the recipient population is very frequently impressed with the naïve approach of its members to sex. The use of contraceptives, which is common in the general population, is a rarity among welfare recipients. It is not that they want more children—in fact the opposite is usually true, but they live in a world where family planning is virtually unknown. In their relationships with the opposite sex, women on welfare sometimes exhibit childlike attitudes of trust. They are not exploited in the real sense or the word, but they are lonely, they have been rejected by a former husband or lover, and they are out to prove, consciously or otherwise, that it was not their fault.

There is, of course, sex in welfare. If someone like the late Dr. Kinsey made a study he would probably conclude that there is about the same amount of sexual activity among welfare recipients as there is in the general population. When one reminds the inquiring taxpayer that extramarital excursions in sex are not exclusive activities of those who receive public assistance, he is apt to reply that he does not mind people having that kind of fun, but he objects to paying for it by taxation. What he is really saying is that there should be two standards of acceptable moral behavior: one for welfare recipients and a different one for the non-recipient population. The affluent businessman who is wise in the ways of contraception and who may indulge in extramarital activities can be among the most bitter of the critics. He may condemn the mothers who receive aid for illegitimate children for emulating his own moral behavior.

Mrs. B was a most attractive divorcée and the mother of four precocious children. Their father was a former minister who had long since disappeared into that anonymous realm where absent fathers go. Mrs. B received aid for herself and her children and seemed to enjoy a varied and exciting life. There was a steady procession of men to her door, and some of them were prominent citizens. The children were very flexible, and they accepted as a matter of course the number of "uncles" who were visitors in the home. One of their favorites was the owner of a Cadillac convertible, who parked the car in the shade and let them play in it while he and the mother made love in the house. His visits, in contrast to most of those by the other "uncles," were always made in the daylight hours. He was the owner of a thriving business and the husband of a demanding and socially prominent wife. While he pursued his activities his wife campaigned vigorously against immorality in welfare. She was persuasive in women's club meetings and other circles but her husband continued to be the favorite "uncle" at the "B" house.

The current interest in the topless image is a bit hard for me to understand, and I have to keep reminding myself that I belong to a past generation. The era in which I grew up might have been designated as the BBB period, because it certainly was Before the Bottle Baby. Children were breast-fed, and anyone who had not witnessed the spectacle of a baby tugging at a full breast would have had to have been a hermit or a recluse. The thought of going to a nightclub and paying to see a bare bosom never occurred to anyone, since a woman's bared breast was just as common a sight as the flag on the Fourth of July.

The majority of mothers of dependent children on welfare are modern by most standards, and the plastic nursing bottle is in common use. There are some, however, who are still old-fashioned, and the topless devotee could get an eyeful in our waiting room any day in the week.

Sex constitutes one of the many hazards of the welfare case-worker's job. Orientation sessions for new workers are featured by warnings to women about older single men and to young men about the perils of visiting women in their homes. The so-called client-caseworker relationship can become quite strained when the young woman worker makes a call with nothing in mind other than an annual investigation and confronts a situation where an amorous male has something entirely different on his mind. Every welfare office has a record of these would-be Don Juans, and in some instances workers visit them in pairs. Age is not always the determining factor in compiling such a list, as some of our senior citizens are the most ardent pursuers.

It is not unusual for the young male caseworker to be accused of making improper advances towards a female recipient of aid. In the vast majority of cases the "pass" exists only in the imagination of the self-described victim, and it may be attempted as a mild form of blackmail to secure fringe financial benefits which are not ordinarily available. On some occasions, male caseworkers invite accusations by sitting on sofas with clients or indiscreetly following them into bedrooms or bathrooms.

One of our young male employees who had only recently been hired returned from a field trip with a look of stark terror on his face. He had been making home calls and was looking for an address. There were audible indications of merriment coming from an apartment, and he knocked on the door. He was invited in with enthusiasm and opened the door to a scene of debauchery such as he had never previously witnessed. The room was a hilarious mixture of adults of both sexes in various poses of nudity, the floor was littered with liquor bottles, and four small children were crawling about. He made an awkward but rapid retreat and came straight back to the office. We called the police and they found the situation as he had described it. The adults went to jail on charges of contributing to the neglect of minors, and the children came to us to be placed in foster homes.

The college girls who come to work for us are usually from

homes with high moral standards, and although modern youth is sophisticated and sex educated, the young girl graduate is not always prepared for what she sees. The seamy side of life is not confined to the area across the tracks, but it is less well hidden there than in the more affluent neighborhoods. One of our caseworkers, calling on recipients in a small hotel, was trying to locate a woman who had applied for aid. The desk clerk rather reluctantly gave her a room number and she knocked on the door several times before it opened to reveal a startling sight. The woman who came to the door was obviously intoxicated, and there were a number of empty and partially filled whiskey bottles on the floor and the dresser. The bed had seen better days, and its center was much lower than its head or foot. A nude male lay on his back on the bed and was oblivious to anything that was going on. Our worker came back to the office determined to resign, and it took some effort to convince her that her experience was not something she could anticipate on a regular basis.

There cannot always be complete assurance that the caseworker calling on one of his own sex will be completely free from the occasional "pass." One of our elderly recipients becomes amorously interested in any young male who calls on him. He is supposed to have limited vision but pays little or no attention when an older man or woman assigned to his case calls at his home.

My first working experience in welfare was as a caseworker and a supervisor in an eastern state. Like most welfare department employees, I had no experience when I went on the job. The department had vacancies, and an unusual law of supply and demand soon elevated me to a position of supervisor, a position for which I was not too well prepared. I was very proud of the people under my supervision and determined to make the unit the best in the department. There was one problem which really plagued me: one of the caseworkers in my unit was a very pleasant and attractive young girl who did a reasonably good job when she was there, but she was very consistently tardy. Although the rest of the office reported for work at eight A.M., she came along at nine or even ten o'clock and seemed to accept her time of arrival as nothing unusual. After speaking to her on several occasions and being answered with nothing more than a knowing smile, I determined that she would have to be fired.

A member of our board of county commissioners came by to see me and in the course of our conversation he inquired about the tardy girl. I knew he was acquainted with her but this did not deter me from telling him that she was always late and that I was going to fire her. His manner suddenly became cold and formal and he looked me right in the eye and said, "I wouldn't do that if I were you." Even though I was young and enthusiastic I realized that there was some kind of message of caution in his words.

A few days later I was conferring with the director of the department and I mentioned my conversation with the county commissioner. The director was more than amused. He asked me if I knew what the score was and when I replied in the negative he said, "Your tardy caseworker is the commissioner's girl friend and he sleeps with her every night. The fact that he didn't fire you on the spot is a mystery to me. You'll probably be with us for a long time."

Recruiting foster homes is a continuous task for welfare departments. There are never enough of them and there is a high turnover rate with a number of them quitting the business for various reasons. Securing foster homes for teenagers is doubly difficult. Many people stand in awe of teenagers, including those who have struggled with children of their own through the difficult years. At the other end of the age scale, the baby is very easy to place, and most foster parents prefer to care for infants or young children.

Mary was a beautiful teen-age girl whose father was deceased and whose mother had long ago drifted off into the world of prostitution and liquor, where there is little to be gained by having a child around. Mary had been a foster home girl since infancy, and like most foster home children, she had lived in many different homes. She was a very affectionate girl and was particularly fond of the men who were her foster fathers. As a child this was well accepted, but as she matured into an attractive young woman with unusual physical endowments a few problems arose. She particularly enjoyed greeting the man of the house when he came home from work, and when he sat in his favorite chair she would recline in his lap and throw her arms around his neck. This might have been an acceptable routine in most of the households if Mary had not insisted on being attired only in panties and brassiere.

The foster home fathers as a whole did not seem to be too upset, but foster home mothers reacted violently, and we would have to move Mary to another home. She finally grew up, married, and moved to a distant city, and we hope she has at last found a home of her own where she can greet the man of the house in her own fashion and without fear of endangering her tenure there.

Contrary to general opinion, mothers who receive aid for dependent minor children have to be good managers to survive. In our large cities, they, of necessity, rent slum dwellings and live on the edge of privation. The mother of hungry children can become desperate, and her concern for her children may lead her to bargain her feminine charms for financial favors. Although some mothers of welfare children do sell their female wares, the wonder is that, living under the economic stress they do, more of them do not resort to prostitution.

I recently became acquainted with an attractive woman who had become an employee in the law office of a long-time friend. She seemed to have an unusual interest in welfare and always inquired about the status of operations in our office. One day when we were conversing about public assistance she told me about her personal experience as a former welfare recipient.

She had lived in a large city and was married—happily, she thought—until after the birth of her first baby, when her husband disappeared. She was not well and was alone without friends or relatives. Her application for welfare became involved in a tangle of bureaucratic error and was delayed. She told me that she had been reared under a strict moral code and had, up to that point, always been a "decent" person. There was no money for milk for the baby. She knew that other girls in the apartment house were call girls and she made her first contact. The baby was left with a neighbor and she went to a motel where the contact appeared shortly thereafter. She was so upset that as she disrobed for her part of the paid performance she told her partner of her situation. He must have had a surge of conscience, for he asked her to dress, gave her ten dollars and left. The welfare check came in a few days, and she soon became strong enough to return to work. She is now supporting herself and the baby. She admits that but for the grace of God, or the conscience of a gentleman, she might have been a call girl in a big city instead of a working mother in a law office.

Every profession develops a language of its own and an array of alphabetical abbreviations to explain its activities. Those of us who work with these symbols are prone to forget that they are not universally known and accepted, and we find ourselves phrasing bureaucratic symbols and slogans which mean very little to anyone else. When medical care for welfare recipients came into being it brought with it a new list of symbolized designations. For the medical needy the symbol became MN; for those lacking residence, LRR (lacks residence requirements); for those who refused a grant of aid, RG (refuses grant); and so on ad infinitum. One of the prerequisites to being a medically needy person was to be "linked" in some way to a welfare eligibility requirement. In other words, in addition to needing medical care and being unable to pay for it, one had to be aged, blind, disabled, or a minor child deprived of support and supervision of a parent.

The spouses of welfare recipients who were not receiving aid themselves had a great deal of difficulty in accepting the fact that they were not considered medically needy and were not eligible for medical care. In attempting to explain this to the wife of a disabled recipient of aid, I had unknowingly lapsed into welfare jargon and had mentioned that linkage to some program was necessary and that she was not linked. She drew a deep breath and told me rather belligerently that she had been married to the same man for more than thirty-five years and if that was not being linked she would like to know what was. Obviously I could not explain a more definite "linkage" than that, but I did realize that the language we talk within our departmental walls frequently means little or nothing to those on the outside.

One of the requirements for receipt of aid for a dependent child is to cooperate with welfare departments and law enforcement officers in identifying and locating the father. The matter of determining who the father is sometimes difficult. There is the occasional loyal girl who may or may not still be in love with the father of her illegitimate child but who protects him even in the face of deprivation. The requirement that the father be identified is not always known to those who are mothers of fatherless children.

A very beautiful young girl with a healthy three-month-old baby came to our office to apply for aid. Her name had been in the papers as a correspondent in a divorce suit which involved one of our best-known and wealthiest ranchers. When the time came to identify the father of her child she at first hesitated and then refused to divulge his name. She said that he was a prominent rancher and that she did not wish to cause him further trouble or embarrassment. When asked how she would support the child, she looked a bit bewildered but said that she would find some way to do it.

The woman who has been more or less promiscuous in her relationships with the opposite sex is sometimes hard-put to name the father of a particular child. On occasion she is unable to do so in spite of her willingness to cooperate to the best of her ability. There are times when she unwillingly or otherwise leads welfare investigators and district attorneys on fruitless searches which terminate with blood tests proving she has to be mistaken.

I well remember one young woman who, having failed to identify the father of her illegitimate child after several attempts, appeared in my office. She now was willing to face the fact that she did not really know who was the father of her child. She and the child were in need and I attempted to help her establish some identity which would satisfy the district attorney. I repeated the necessity for her to make every attempt to name the father of her child and asked her if there was something she might have forgotten. Could she describe him? She could not. She did not know his name, address or nickname. It was obvious that we were not going to establish paternity and I was about ready to terminate the interview when her face lighted up and she said, "I remember something! The number of his truck was 13."

Our stress on civil rights and the concern for the alleged or suspected offender has changed our *modus operandi* as far as night calls are concerned. Our night calls used to be made at any or all hours. We entered the house on invitation only, and one investigator stationed himself at the back door to apprehend any departing guests. Our methods remain essentially the same except that we are now required to limit our calls to the early evening and morning hours. We also go to elaborate lengths to inform people of their rights.

In the course of a few years our investigators have happened on some intimate and embarrassing scenes. It seems, for instance, to take an unusually long time for an errant male to don his pants when women and children are present and the investigators are waiting to lead him away to the local bastille. A lone man fleeing out the back door or window *sans* the usual attire will startle even the most experienced investigator who is waiting to apprehend him.

One of the most startling things about night calls is the fact that investigators are voluntarily admitted to the house without a search warrant when the body of the crime is still in residence. The number of times when we are denied entrance is very insignificant. Our critics are quick to point out that there is an implied threat in our very presence and they have also indicated that we are less than gentle in our approach to the subject matter at hand. Our investigators are well trained and thoroughly schooled on the exact procedures to be followed in gaining entrance to the home of a welfare recipient, and in my experience there have been few instances where courtesy and regard for the other person's rights were not displayed. There will continue to be arguments about this, and I am quite convinced that at sometime in the not too distant future our concern for the rights of the suspected will result in the elimination of night calls at the homes of welfare recipients. At this point in time we will have to ignore the man in the house who is there without license.

It is frequently pointed out to us that were we to make nocturnal visits to all residences of nonrecipients where there is an illegal bed partner enjoying the comforts and privileges of the home, our investigative staff would have to be increased many times over. Our critics claim that we would not do this very long because of the prominence of some of the habitués of the bedrooms, and I cannot argue with this point.

There is a general belief that many women who are welfare recipients are also actively engaged in the world's oldest profession. Actually there are few welfare women who do engage in prostitution. The surprising thing is that there are not many more who fall before the temptation of money and clothing to supplement a meager existence. Anyone who has observed prostitution will refute the prevalent notion that its basic motivations for women are lust and desire for sexual activity. Prostitution from the woman's viewpoint is built upon economics. If we were to insure all practicing prostitutes a secure and adequate income, the male population would have to look elsewhere for its sexual gratification.

Mothers of dependent children who live on the thin edge of privation, whose families are usually inadequately housed and poorly fed with the monthly allowances they receive from welfare, must be among the most sorely tempted when opportunities arise to sell their sexual wares. In the big urban centers, where most of them by necessity must rear their families in the slums, it would be difficult to condemn them for attempting to improve their financial situations. Many women under conditions with less financial stress have joined the "sisters of sin" for monetary gain.

A few wags sitting on the sidelines and observing the increasing services available to welfare recipients have suggested that "sexicare" be added to Medicare and the other fringe benefits which are a part of welfare programs. Their suggestions seldom evolve into details and it is difficult to determine exactly what they have in mind. In general they, along with a host of others, view welfare as a huge melting pot of sex with clandestine relationships and illegitimate babies as the order of the day. They would be most disappointed to know that sex in welfare is just about as important and prevalent as it is outside welfare, and were its recipients granted more reasonable and secure standards of assistance it would be even less important than it actually is.

Chapter VIII

Lonesome Road

THE SCRIPTURES mark a special place in heaven for children. This is in distinct contrast to the plight of many children here on earth, particularly those supported by public welfare. They experience want while surrounded by those who have plenty. Our legislators give recognition to the needs of dependent children but not in the same manner or measure as they do for the needy aged. This disparity is frequently and accurately explained by the assertion that "kids don't vote." A glaring example in program differences for the aged and the children is the fact that legislators have increased grants to the aged on the basis that the cost of living has risen but they have not recognized this fact in the amounts of money granted to dependent children.

At the other end of life's spectrum, the aged are better cared for in material ways but are denied the love and attention they crave. Taken together, the children and aged who are on welfare represent a lonely segment of our population. The majority of the children have been rejected by at least one parent. Many of the aged have been cast aside by their families and virtually forgotten.

The most lonely of the children dwell in an uncertain existence in foster homes. The aged, whose families are either unwilling or unable to care for them, spend their last years in the secluded loneliness of rest homes and nursing homes. Visit a foster home and you will see the hunger for affection and the desperate search for something which is not to be obtained. The children receive good physical care and quite frequently warmth and affection. They have, however, been rejected by fathers and mothers and this has left an indelible mark on their outlook towards life.

A visit to a nursing home is like a rendezvous with impending death. Everything is sheer white—the walls, the fixtures and, most of all, the stark faces staring at space or achieving temporary release in slumber. The care in the majority of nursing homes is excellent. The nurses and assistants are cheerful and devoted to their patients. The real sadness is that there is so little hope. This, for many, is the last stop on the way to eternity. In their dreams, and during periods of flight from consciousness, they mumble incoherently about going home. In their waking and conscious hours they realize that there is no home to which to return and no relatives willing or able to receive them, yet they cling to hope. A visit with them makes it difficult to mourn sudden death.

Our children in foster homes and our aged parents in rest homes and nursing homes have suffered the pangs of rejection. They have lost the security which results from being accepted as a member of a closely knit group. Children in foster homes are most conscious of this. They are torn between the extremes of love and hate and are bewildered. They sense rejection with a keen awareness. They admit it only to themselves in their strange beds, in the stillness of the lonely night. Human nature being what it is, they accept the blame for rejection, reasoning that there is something wrong with them which brought about the separation from their parents. The social worker who by chance mentions the parents in derogatory terms commits a fatal mistake. To talk about the mother in negative terms is to condemn the child, for the child is part and parcel of its parents, and if they are condemned, so is the child.

Foster home care is frequently hailed as the answer to the neglected and delinquent child's problems. Those of us who have experienced the emotional pulls which the foster home child endures would refute this assertion. They are at best a substitute for a normal and natural home. They are transient in existence and many foster home children move almost constantly. This is particularly true of children who are bed wetters and who have emotional problems. It is also characteristic of the behavior-problem child and the teenager.

In our search for foster homes we seek the ideal and frequently settle for much less. We pay foster home parents a pittance and expect them to perform miracles of devotion and problem solving.

On occasion we attempt to place in foster homes children who are so emotionally wounded that they cannot relate to anyone. These children hate with a vengeance beyond description, and they trust no one. Many of them are on the edge of psychopathic behavior and will grow up to join the criminal offenders who wage war against society. To accomplish the near-impossible task of working with difficult children, we seek only those who have pure motives. Those who expect a reasonable monetary return for their time and effort are summarily rejected. We have been reared on a tradition that foster home care should be provided out of the goodness of foster parents' hearts. As a result we usually get just about what we pay for. It would seem to be much more sensible to select, train, and adequately compensate a professional corps of foster home parents.

Traditional patterns in the criteria for selection of foster home parents are hard to break, but there is evidence of some break-through. In Chicago, good results have been obtained from foster homes where the age-old requirement of two parents has been waived. The concept of two parents is ideal, but there are fathers and mothers who have by themselves maintained homes charac-terized by love, compatibility, and happy children.

At the time a child is placed in a foster home he has not only been rejected by his parents but frequently by the community as well. Leo was eight years of age. He had been a resident of a county detention home for a year and received, as a doubtful gift, a commitment to a correctional school on his eighth birthday. There was no record of his ever having been delinquent, but he had become a nuisance and a blot on the conscience of the small town where he lived. His father had deserted the family many years before and his mother was an alcoholic. He foraged for food in garbage cans and begged on the streets. There were no foster homes available, and the juvenile judge determined that his situa-tion would be improved by a commitment to the county detention home.

When he arrived at the correctional school he came to the at-tention of a kind and understanding superintendent. Leo was small for his age, and as his eyes darted about he appeared to re-semble a frightened rabbit more than a delinquent boy. The superintendent soon determined that he had no place among the sophisticated delinquents who inhabited the institution. He got in touch with the local welfare office and asked that Leo be placed in a foster home.

The social workers who supervise children in foster home care have a most difficult and frequently thankless task. They are constantly tugged at by the conflicting emotions and interests of the natural parents, the foster home parents, and the child. The daily dramas which they witness make a constant drain on their emotions. Of all the tasks in public welfare, theirs is the most difficult.

The social worker who was assigned to locate a foster home for Leo and to be responsible for his supervision was an extraordinary person. She loved children, and at the same time she understood them. On the day Leo became her charge, there were no foster homes immediately available. She broke all the ancient and honored taboos of foster care by taking him into her home that night. On the way to her home she purchased material to make soap bubbles. Leo blew soap bubbles with a great deal of joy, but he did not attempt to catch them as most children are prone to do. He waited until they hovered above the ground and then, with shouts of glee, stomped them into the earth. Here at last was something on which he could vent his feelings. When the caseworker tucked him in bed and kissed him goodnight, he said he felt "all warm inside."

The next day Leo was taken to a foster home operated by an exceptional couple. They had devoted their lives to rearing foster children, and their "family" had grown over the years. As boys and girls grew into young adulthood, they left to make their own lives and were replaced by new arrivals like Leo. He seemed to accept his placement in the home, but his behavior was sometimes erratic. He could not be left alone with smaller children, and the foster mother and a pediatrician watched him with interest and fear. The good doctor spent an unusual amount of time playing with Leo and the other children. The slightest provocation could trigger a violent temper tantrum on Leo's part, and he was prone to assault younger children. One day the foster mother reached out in time to prevent him from hitting a baby over the head with a baseball bat.

In spite of these difficulties the foster mother thought she could eventually win Leo over with affection. The doctor had discovered some deep-seated scars on his head which appeared to have been afflicted with heavy, blunt instruments. It was his medical opinion that Leo had been repeatedly struck on the head and that there was a possibility of brain damage.

Three years went by with Leo's behavior patterns showing signs of steady deterioration. The foster mother was loath to give up but finally conceded that Leo was beyond her help. He was sent to a mental institution for observation and was found to be psychotic. The wounds inflicted by his parents and the community left scars which had never really healed. He was committed for permanent care and will spend the rest of his life as a ward of the state. He became a permanent member of that community whose citizens continuously dwell outside the realms of reality.

Not all the neglected children are in foster homes. In and out of welfare homes children are abused and in some instances beaten and maimed for life by their parents. The battered-child syndrome is receiving a great deal of attention. It is by no means a new phenomenon; we have just become more conscious of it. Medical people and others have become more vocal in expressing themselves about conditions which have existed for a long time.

Years ago, my experience with children in foster home care caused me to be loaned to a domestic relations court for certain cases. These were instances where both parents wanted the children. It might be more acurate to say that each parent did not want the other to have the children. These were cases when the cups of bitter hatred had overflowed. The judge needed help in deciding the best thing to be done about the children. I had the task of making studies and recommendations on which he could base his judgment; this was a difficult thing to do. Each parent had nothing but evil to say about the other. Each had also gathered a following of relatives and friends who echoed his or her sentiments. In many instances the children would have been better off away from both parents. This, however, was a rare decision for the court to make.

I recall one case where there were extreme emotional feelings on the part of both parents. Each one had asked for custody of five minor children, and the court directed me to make a recommendation as to which parent should be awarded custody. I talked with many of the couple's friends and relatives and gathered a host of positive and negative opinions about each one. When the day of the court hearing arrived, the mother, who had been awarded temporary custody, brought all five children to the courtroom. After a lengthy and bitterly contested hearing the judge awarded custody to the father. The children screamed hysterically and clung to their mother. A bailiff forcibly took them from her and gave them to the father. I never saw any of the family after that. I have often wondered if the children were ever able to really recover from the effects of the courtroom drama. In divorce actions, husbands and wives are hurt, but children are frequently damaged beyond recovery.

There is seldom a night that passes in our city without an instance of child neglect coming to the official attention of police and sheriff's officers. Children are left alone in automobiles while their parents party inside some night spot. More frequently they are left alone at home while fathers and mothers, or parents and paramours, make the rounds of the bars. It is a shocking experience for young children to be left without supervision. It is very disturbing to be taken from home and placed in a receiving home or an institution.

Our social workers who are in charge of foster home care are assigned to emergency duty on a rotating basis. This tour of responsibility continues for one week. During this time they are assigned a county car and must be available by telephone twenty-four hours a day, including weekends and holidays. When law enforcement officers find abandoned or neglected children, they take them to the hospital and call our workers. These calls come at any hour. Our workers meet the children at the hospital and take them to a temporary receiving home. The children are upset, and by the time they are settled in the receiving home most of the night has passed. This is a difficult experience for the children and it is not an easy one for our workers. They get no extra compensation and little thanks. The attention they get for this extra duty quite frequently consists of calls from irate taxpayers. They have observed the county cars being operated after hours and have concluded that they are being used for unofficial business.

Society is most inconsistent in its attitudes towards children. For voting purposes an eighteen-year-old is a child. For military purposes he is an adult. From the viewpoint of agencies operating foster home programs the eighteen-year-old has suddenly become self-sufficient and economically independent. After years of close supervision and care he is suddenly on his own. Foster home care is terminated at age eighteen.

Victor was eighteen years of age and was released on his own to return to a situation which had always been intolerable. He was a shy, handsome Negro boy who had been adopted in infancy by Spanish parents. They were told that his father was Indian and his mother Irish. As he grew into childhood it was evident that someone had been mistaken. When he became a teen-ager his adoptive mother died. His father was elderly and ill and was unable to care for himself or Victor. They moved to the home of the father's oldest son and into a situation where Victor was very unwelcome.

He had been reared in a small town where he was considered to be an unnecessary nuisance. As soon as his Negroid characteristics developed, his family rejected him and the community followed suit. He was extremely proud of his ability to speak Spanish and would not consider himself a Negro.

Philip Nolan was fictionally a man without a country. Victor was literally a boy without a friend. The Caucasians ignored him and the Spanish boys deliberately shunned him. The Negroes stood in awe of his ability with the Spanish language and would have nothing to do with him. He made many attempts to associate with Spanish boys of his own age but was rebuffed on every occasion.

In his senior year at high school he allegedly stole a dollar from a locker. This gave his adoptive brother and the community a chance for which they had been waiting. They moved swiftly, and Victor was summarily committed to a correctional school for boys. While he was in the facility a well-meaning counselor told him that he was a Negro and would have to accept the fact. Victor became hysterical and had to be placed under sedation.

After a relatively short stay in the institution, Victor was released with the stipulation that he be placed in a foster home. The child welfare worker who had the responsibility for finding a suitable foster home was in a quandary. The institutional parole officer had recommended that Victor be placed in a Negro foster home. After reviewing the disastrous results of attempting to force his Negro heritage upon him, the worker decided to place him with Spanish people. Victor was not happy. In spite of all the difficulties, he wanted to be with his father. He requested weekly visiting privileges but was only permitted to go on occasion.

One weekend when he was home the local jewelry store was burglarized. The safe had been drilled and the door blown off with a charge of nitroglycerine. It had all the earmarks of a professional job. When the burglary was discovered early the next morning, the chief of police promptly arrested Victor as the number-one suspect. He was mortally afraid of firecrackers, but the local police had to have a suspect, and he was it. Needless to say, he knew no more about the burglary than the chief of police did.

On his eighteenth birthday he returned home to find the situation as impossible as ever. His father attempted to be kind to him but his adoptive brother and sister-in-law were determined to be rid of him. After a few weeks he realized the futility of attempting to remain in his adoptive brother's house. He joined the Navy to get away from an intolerable situation. He became a "career man" and may have finally found some degree of acceptance.

The welfare laws of some states permit the mother of dependent children to have a bed partner without benefit of marriage. This is typical of some of our welfare laws which are supposedly for dependent children but which place their primary concern with the mother and her desire for extramarital affairs. Many of these relationships are transient and casual. The children accept the visitors as "uncles." Children, however, are much more sophisticated than adults usually think. They know what the situation is, and they are chagrined. If they attempt to forget it, their companions on the schoolgrounds refresh their memories. Some welfare workers would require the mother to choose between her clandestine affairs and aid for her children. Those with this view are promptly termed "moralists" by others, who point to the common-law arrangements in all levels of society.

The seasoned observer may or may not be a "moralist" but he sees ample evidence of damage to children. The father has previously left the children, and when the mother turns to a strange man it is interpreted by the children as further parental rejection. The younger children adjust better to the mother's arrangements than do the older ones. As girls reach puberty they have before them an example of promiscuity and casual relationships. Teenage boys do not accept the dominant role of a natural father with ease. They reject and resent the household position assumed by the mother's latest friend. In far too many instances, girls in common-law households become pregnant without benefit of marriage. Boys frequently leave home and rush into unsatisfactory marriages. The offspring are dependent children who will be added to the welfare rolls. The oft-repeated assertion that welfare flows down through the second and third generation is all too frequently true. Given the home situations in which many welfare children live, it is a miracle that more of them do not repeat the failures of their parents.

Pension promoters and well-meaning relatives have worked a cruel hoax on the needy aged. To further their own financial interests the promoters have repeatedly told the elderly that Old Age Assistance is not welfare but a "pension." Relatives who, if Old Age Assistance were not available, would be required to support their parents and grandparents cover their feelings of guilt by referring to the "pension." This makes it difficult for the elderly person who is the recipient of aid from a most complicated public assistance program. He thinks of the "pension" as a flat amount and cannot accept the monetary fluctuations which occur in 40 per cent of the grants each month. Many of the elderly sincerely believe that a welfare worker has pocketed the amount by which his "pension" has been reduced.

Mr. Jay's assistance grant had been reduced by five dollars. He had been allowed that amount each month to purchase a refrigerator. Payment was now completed but Mr. Jay was vigorously protesting the reduction in his pension. He came into my office for a high-level explanation. I gave him the same one his caseworker did. Our conversation drifted from his current monetary situation to "old times." He had lived a most interesting life and I was fascinated by his stories about early times in our community. I thought he had forgotten about the "pension" aspect, but as he got ready to leave he said; "You've been polite, and I've enjoyed talking with you, but I want to tell you something. The next time you run for the office of welfare director, I'm not going to vote for you."

Whenever I return to the office after an absence of a few days, my assistant and my secretary brief me on what has happened. Invariably they tell me that "Several of your little old men and women called, but they didn't want to talk to us. They'll be calling again."

As time has permitted, I have, for several years, listened to some of the elderly who have no one else to talk to. It does not require much conversation on my part. Mostly, I just listen, sometimes to stories and happenings which I have heard many times before. There are times when I do paper work at my desk while I listen. I am not being impolite or inattentive, for I have learned to work and listen at the same time. My aged callers are lonely people. Some of them have relatives and friends, but this is a busy world. Our time for listening seems to lessen with the years.

I have never met some of my callers, and Mrs. Green is one of these. She tells me what a beautiful young woman she was and how attractive she was to the opposite sex. She recounts intimate details of her physical ills and her visits to the doctor. She lives near the welfare office and accuses me of something to which I cannot plead guilty: "Every night I see you working," she insists. "Your office lights are on until eleven o'clock." I tell her that I go home around five P.M. and that the lights she sees are left on until the janitors finish cleaning the building. I might as well save my breath; she is convinced that I am a slave and that I am working myself to death. There is nothing I can say which will change her mind.

Not all of the lonely aged reside in nursing homes. Anyone who visits the small-hotel section of any large city will see ample evidence of lonesome road.

On a recent visit to Los Angeles I spent an evening walking through a part of the city where small hotels abound. Not all of the guests were aged, but most of them seemed to be. The aged sat in front of windows facing the street. They rocked and stared as the busy world went by.

The next morning was as beautiful as only Los Angeles can be. The sun was shining brightly, the air was crisp and cool, and there was no smog. I decided to walk from my hotel room to the building where a series of meetings were to be held. My route took me through the area I had visited the previous evening. The streets were almost deserted except for a few elderly men and women. They were walking alone and appeared to be oblivious to everything around them. As each one approached, I observed that they were engaged in earnest conversation, and I first thought they were speaking to me. I soon realized that they were addressing no one in particular. Living in hotel rooms in a large city, I could only surmise that there was no one to listen to them, but they talked anyway. I do not recall the name of the street, but for the aged it was apparently the street of dreams.

As I walked up Broadway somone was shouting in a voice audible above all the noise of the city. Walking ahead of me was an elderly man who at frequent intervals gave vent to loud but unintelligible statements. I kept pace with him for several blocks. There were a few curious onlookers but most people walked on without even appearing to notice the self-appointed town crier. When he reached a large public building, he climbed to the top step. He poured out a voluminous barrage of words which could be heard for some distance but which were jumbled and meaningless. In a few moments the guardians of the law arrived and gently led him away. He had been alone too long and was attempting to tell someone about it. He has probably joined the ranks of the senile psychotic in some mental facility. If so, he will not be alone, for our mental institutions contain many senior citizens who have drifted away from the world of reality.

Uncle, as many of us call him, is a delightful character. He lives alone in his little house and has maintained an unusual degree of independence. He has definite opinions on many subjects and he loves any side of a controversial discussion. I went to visit him on one occasion and found him absorbed in the daily news-paper. His feet were perched on a table in characteristic pose. A burned-out cigar stub dangled at an uncertain angle from the corner of his mouth. The room as usual was dusty and cluttered. I thought Uncle was reading without passion, but he suddenly struck the table a dust-dispensing blow. "That ought to be a felony," he shouted, "by God, that ought to be a felony." When I inquired as to what heinous offense should rank as a felony, he shoved the newspaper into my hands and said; "Putting that wom-an's picture in the newspaper." Uncle was a staunch Republican and his ire had been raised by a large picture of the First Lady presiding at a White House luncheon.

A few days later he called to invite me to come and see him. It was mid-morning and my desk was stacked with work which had to be done. When I told him that I was busy he became impatient. I reminded him that I had a job to do and asked if he had any-thing special in mind. "I want you to help me start a new church," he said. I told him that I had many things to do and could not sit around all day, organizing a new religion. "What do you mean, all day?" he replied with great indignation. "You damned fool, we can beat anything in existence in fifteen minutes!" Old age would be fun if all of us could retain Uncle's interest in life and his sense of humor.

Some aged persons are alone even in the last earthly rites. To some, death is an uneventful escape from the pangs of solitude. Juan was alone in his later years and virtually alone when death came. He achieved notoriety after he died, in contrast to his ob-scure life.

One of our social workers had visited the nursing home where Juan had passed away. The visit was at the request of the owner of the home. She told our worker that in his death throes, Juan had vomited heavily. When she and her daughter attended the brief funeral services which the county requires for the indigent dead, they were not permitted to view his body. They followed the hearse to potter's field and again demanded to see him. The driver of the hearse finally relented. The brief view revealed Juan in his underwear, badly stained from his final spell of vomiting.

The county has sparse but definite requirements for burial of its indigent dead. "Suitable burial clothing" is one of the stipulations in the contract with undertakers. If the story were true, this was a serious violation of the agreement with the county and would have to be investigated. I asked the social worker to have the owner of the nursing home put her statements in writing. When he returned with an affidavit stating that Juan had been buried in soiled underwear, I knew something had to be done.

Burial of the indigent dead was a responsibility of our department, but disinterment was another matter. I called the district attorney, and he told me that the grave would have to be opened. He issued an order which directed me to have the grave opened and the corpse viewed. I called the superintendent of the cemetery and made the necessary arrangements. It was also necessary to request that the health department take possession of the body and keep it in cold storage pending further disposition.

The scene at the grave site was the most unusual and certainly the most eerie I have ever witnessed. I had asked that the president of the funeral directors' association, the sheriff's photographer and other witnesses be present. As we stood in the dry sand around the grave, the workmen were scraping the last dirt off the casket. One of my assistants, who accompanied me, had worked in a mortuary while attending school. He climbed down into the grave and removed the lid from the casket. There lay Juan, as he had been buried, in his stained underwear. My assistant determined that the body had been embalmed, and the photographer took a number of pictures. The board of supervisors was in session and I went to the courthouse to report to them. They determined that the matter should be formally heard at a special hearing.

The next few days were among the most difficult I have every experienced. The funeral director was a prominent and well-respected man. The special hearing would be an occasion highly charged with emotion. Television and all other news media would be there, and they would make the most of it. I had only recently been appointed to my position. I did not have a personal acquaintance with any member of the board, and they had given me no indication of how they felt or what they would do. A number of emissaries called at my office before the hearing. One of them, in particular, reminded me of the prominence of the funeral director. He rather pointedly let me know that I was not too well known. He mildly suggested that maybe I would like to "back off." I thought the chances of losing my job were good, but I was determined to go through with the hearing, regardless of the circumstances.

The board room was packed for the hearing. As I recounted the circumstances under which Juan was buried, the photographer passed pictures of the opened casket to the board members and the news media. The majority of the board members were noncommittal, but one member, who was a personal friend of the funeral director, was righteously indignant. He said that in spite of the pictures, he did not believe that such a fine man had done anything wrong.

I fully expected the undertaker to blame the matter on an oversight by a subordinate. Instead he said that the deceased did not have any friends or relatives and was only an old Mexican. He concluded his statement by saying that he did not make any money out of indigent burials anyway.

As I look at the account of the hearing in yellowed newspaper clippings, I realize that I might have done better if I had retained my composure. Four members of the board continued to sit in silence and my resentment got the better of me. It appeared to me that they were willing to hush the matter up. I told them that if that was their desire they could get themselves a new welfare director forthwith. My conclusions were a little premature; the four members of the board stated that the matter had been handled exactly right. They commended me with a vote of thanks and confidence. To the surprise of everyone the former lone dissenter joined in the vote to make it unanimous.

The funeral director was suspended from participating in indigent burials for a period of time. The board ordered welfare department employees to attend indigent burials in the future and to view the bodies to determine if they were properly clothed for their journey into the great beyond.

Children and the aged who are recipients of welfare are frequently lonely. Those who have family ties are more fortunate than those who have to be cared for by strangers in nursing and foster home facilities. The aged, however, are a more potent political force than our children, and welfare programs for our senior citizens reflect this political significance. In recent years, attempts have been made to organize adult recipients of the children's program. While organizational efforts on the aged level have been most successful, those aimed at the children's program have been uniformly unsuccessful. In general they have been led by outsiders primarily interested in their own financial and political gains. The recipients have been led to believe that they were a potent political force. The facts of the matter are that the membership in the children's program makes a complete statistical change every three years. No group has ever achieved political muscle with such a rapid turnover in membership.

The tactics of the would-be organizers of the children's program recipients make an interesting study. To anyone who has encountered the far right, the similarity of the approach by the welfare rights organizations is startling. The organizers themselves would be the most startled of all if this were pointed out to them. They approach all discussions in a similar manner. They assume that they are the only honest individuals in existence. They make every attempt to provoke anger and they are frequently rude and overbearing in manner. The objectives of the far righters and the welfare righters differ, but their methods are so similar that a harried public official could close his eyes and have difficulty in identifying his antagonists.

The name *senior citizen* commands attention and respect. The title *welfare rights* provokes resentment and negative reactions. No public relations firm would have chosen welfare rights as the name for a successful organization. It is certainly elementary to point out that welfare recipients do have rights. The facts of life are that the public simply is not ready for such an organizational designation.

In the welfare field, one's thoughts and sympathies go most strongly to those who are beginning and ending life. It is difficult to share more concern with one than the other. It is also difficult, however, to understand the different views which the public has towards needy children and needy aged. The average citizen sees little good in a program to aid dependent children and their mothers. The Old Age Assistance program is, however, a popular

one. Welfare department employees experience difficulty in accepting the transformation which apparently takes place when
the mother of dependent minor children becomes the senior citizen. A sizeable percentage of those who receive Old Age Assistance today were aided yesterday because they were mothers of
dependent children. Like wine, the mothers are apparently trans-
formed by the aging process. Even with the change in status,
many of them must also spend their last years on the uncharted
turns of life's lonesome road.

Chapter IX

Sine Die

THE MILLS of the legislature grind slow, but not so exceedingly fine where welfare is concerned. Each year the state legislatures meet and consider a host of measures concerned with public welfare. The majority of the bills considered and passed either establish new programs or liberalize in some manner those already in existence.

Welfare directors and their assistants give vent to sighs of relief when the legislators finally adjourn. It is indeed a trying period and one featured by contradictions. On the home front the people are demanding less welfare. On the legislative front the senators and assemblymen are approving welfare measures as though they fear public assistance might go out of style. The "good old taxpayer" seldom seems to make any connection between increasing welfare costs and the activities of the legislature. He is much more prone to condemn local authorities and to blame welfare for all his woes.

Under such circumstances it is difficult to remain on an even keel. One has to keep pinching himself to make sure that he has not become afflicted with double hearing. The ear turned towards the home front registers the broken-record plea for the elimination of welfare. The other ear, which is recording the activities of the current session of the legislature, is hearing something entirely different. There are times when one thinks that only the conservatives speak at home and the liberals are vocal only at the legislative level.

The majority of local officials, including welfare directors, are by necessity conservative in their actions. They are forced to do this by the tide of conservative opinion voiced locally. There is also one other compelling reason: if a welfare director gets in trouble for voicing liberal viewpoints, the conservatives attack him, and the liberals refuse to defend him by remaining silent. If he leans to the conservative side, the conservatives praise him and the liberals snipe at him. The public-relations-conscious welfare director soon learns where the most tenable sanctuary is.

The atmosphere of the capitol itself seems to exert a different influence on some people. One of our most conservative county supervisors became an outspoken liberal when he was elected to the state legislature. From an attitude of questioning the purchase of four desks, he became an advocate of more liberal welfare laws. When he was questioned about his change of heart, he said that when he arrived in the capital city he saw the "big picture." There is no doubt that whatever he saw was coming over a different channel than the one to which he had been tuned on the local level. Whatever it was, it certainly changed his attitude towards the expenditure of public funds.

A visit to a legislative session is enough to shake one's faith in the democratic process. From the galleries there appears to be nothing but a great deal of confusion. Measures costing millions of dollars are voted on by the push of a desk button. On many occasions the button pusher is looking the other way or is engaged in lively conversations with several of his colleagues. The casual observer gets the impression that the average legislator pushes the button without always understanding the full impact of the measure on which he is voting.

Some weeks after the close of a session of the legislature, one of our most distinguished representatives called. One of his constituents had complained about the granting of aid in a household where there was a common-law spouse. When I informed him that the legislature had passed the law providing for assistance in such circumstances, he was astounded. "The hell we did!" he said. When I told him that he had voted for the measure, he was more than surprised. "Well, I'll be goddamned!" he said.

There is no doubt that the successful legislator knows where the votes lie. A veteran assemblyman form a notoriously conservative district was known for his liberal voting record. When I remarked that he seemed to vote contrary to the wishes of his constituents, he remarked that I was not a politician. "The organized groups want more welfare," he said. "All of my constitutents have a parent or relative getting help and they don't want the situation to change. They complain about welfare, but they don't vote that way." He must have had the right answer, for he has been reelected many times.

Each year when the legislative session begins, one can expect certain things to happen. Shortly after the session opens, some brave conservative soul will introduce a bill to permit liens on the property of welfare recipients. Someone else will author a measure designed to make public welfare a state (rather than county) administrative responsibility. There will be a rash of measures on the "if and when" basis. These make rather startling suggestions for changes in state law "if and when" the Federal government enacts such enabling legislation.

The authors of all these bills realize that their defeat is a foregone conclusion. They are popular with certain groups and they are introduced to please those groups. This too is good politics, but it clutters up the legislative hoppers and costs the taxpayer a considerable amount of money.

There are occasions when a situation affecting a minimum number of individuals results in an important change in the law. A number of years ago one of the counties in our state changed its property assessment policies. In a county with a population of 1.5 million persons, the change in assessment policies resulted in making two persons ineligible for Old Age Assistance. The legislature reacted immediately. An emergency measure was passed by the legislature and signed by the governor. It doubled the amount of real property an aged person in our state could possess and still be a recipient of Old Age Assistance.

Every year when the legislature meets, some enterprising reporter comes out with a story which announces that there are an unusual number of call girls in the capital city. The legislators rise up with indignation and denounce the story and its author. The bellboys in the hotels are prone to agree with the reporters. If one were looking for the most reliable source of information, he would have to go along with the bellhops.

Prostitution has always followed large gatherings of the opposite sex. This is true of lodge and service club meetings and even large church conventions. When the legislators, the lobbyists, the influence peddlers, and others meet, it is reasonable to expect that call girls will also be in the same location, furthering their particular financial interests.

I was the recipient of a personal experience in the capital city which I strongly suspect was prompted by some of my colleagues. I had just left a number of my fellow directors at the hotel and was walking towards the capitol, when I noticed a young lady approaching. She was looking at me and smiling. I thought for a moment that I might know her, but a second glance convinced me that she was a stranger and I turned my eyes away. As I stopped for a traffic light I was aware of someone standing very near me. I looked up and there was the girl with the friendly smile. "How would you like to come up to my room with me?" she inquired. I was very startled and my reply was somewhat hasty and formal. "Oh no, thank you," I replied. Either my manner or my reply, or both, greatly amused her. She walked on down the street laughing heartily. My colleagues did not ask me any direct questions. They did, however, ask me if I had heard about the influx of call girls, and they exchanged knowing glances. I am quite sure they had a little fun at my expense.

Among those who follow the activities of the legislature there are many pertinent observations about the activities of the lawmakers. One of these is to the effect that there is more legislation planned and approved in certain popular bars than in the halls of the legislature. A visit to a few of these night spots is apt to convince one of the wisdom of the observation. The legislators are there and so are the lobbyists and advocates. They are enjoying themselves, but they are engaged most of the time in serious discussion. An attentive barfly could probably predict with considerable accuracy a major portion of the next day's legislative activities.

In committee hearings, and particularly those which are concerned with interim studies, the legislators flex their muscles and reveal the raw power they possess. If the most adroit person stubs his toe while testifying before them, they will pick his bones. They have humbled the most ardent welfare pension promoters. On occasion they have routed lobbyists and sent them scurrying into the halls.

I was testifying before an interim committee of the legislature. My subject was that section of the law which permits common-law relationships to be recognized in welfare situations. I had documented some seventy-five cases which I thought demonstrated the negative effect on children of the common-law relationship. Immediately following my testimony, the late George McLain was scheduled to address the committee.

I had spent a great deal of time in preparing for the hearing and thought I had a convincing argument. It was obvious that I was not getting over to the committee. There were side conversations among the committee members. One of the members was a long-time acquaintance and he was trying to be attentive. During the course of the testimony, one of his colleagues passed him a note. At the conclusion of my testimony there were no questions. The chairman, attempting to break a noticeable silence, said, "Well, that is quite a story."

It was obvious that the committee was anxious to hear Mr. Mc-Lain. When the hearing closed, my acquaintance came down from the stand to engage me in conversation. "Would you like to see that note I received?" he asked. When I replied in the affirmative he gave me the note. It was evidently scrambled in haste, but its meaning was crystal clear. My effectiveness with the committee was evident as I read: "This guy has fifty votes, maybe. Let's get on with McLain; he has six hundred thousand."

The triumvirate of governmental agencies which administer welfare in many states constitutes the perfect setting for a great deal of buck-passing. Some legislators are prone to deny any responsibility for welfare when approached by a critical constituent. They point the offending finger at the Federal government or the county. State officials complain about Federal dominance and county inefficiency, and counties point the finger at Washington and the state capital. This is all very convenient at times but it must be most confusing to the complaining constituent.

To one who is witness, for the first time, to the closing hours of a legislative session, it appears to be composed entirely of frivolity and chaos. Actually there is a considerable amount of both. In the waning moments, the clock receives a major share of attention. There are struggles over and around it. Some are attempting to turn its hands ahead while others are equally as determined to halt the progression of time. There are always a few who have laid in a store of firecrackers for the occasion. The noise and the smoke from cigarettes and firecrackers further add to a scene of unrealistic drama. A considerable amount of immature behavior is exhibited and a host of pent-up tensions are released. The session finally adjourns, sine die, and the scenes of activity give way to the custodians, who tirelessly gather up the paper airplanes and the spent firecrackers. The noise, confusion and the drama are prone to make one agree with the aged clerk, who has seen many sessions come and go. He slowly shakes his head and with visible feeling says, "Thank God, the legislature meets only once a year."

Although the actions of the legislature give ulcers to administrators and headaches to taxpayers, those who are responsible for welfare management have thrown a few curves past legislators. The history of public welfare in the United States has been marked by predictions and promises, many of which have failed to materialize. Welfare administrators have been the authors of many of these, and their records in the area of crystal gazing have been rather dismal. Most of these unfulfilled promises are forgotten ghosts, but welfare administrators, particularly at Federal and state levels, continue to make rash predictions about newly proposed welfare legislation.

Those states which have adopted the aid-to-stepchildren policy have inherited a necessary recognition of the common-law relationship. Legislators considering these measures have been told that together with Aid to the Unemployed, they would operate to reduce desertion. The number and percentage of children receiving aid because of the desertion of a parent continues to increase. It would take much more imagination than the average person possesses to observe any fulfillment of the promises made about a reduction in desertions.

The United States Congress had been so thoroughly convinced of the promised savings in the welfare "Services" program that one year after its implementation it reduced—and later hastily restored—the Federal appropriation for public welfare. While the

"Services" program may be justified for other reasons, any thinking welfare administrator knows that its full implementation means more, not less, expenditure of funds.

There are other examples of promises and predictions about welfare which have not been fulfilled by experience. If legislators and congressmen have memories and recollections, they must look at public welfare and its promises with varying degrees of skepticism. New and expanded welfare programs may be necessary and desirable but it is abundantly clear that they do not hold the answer to the reduction of public welfare's increasing case loads.

During every legislative session there are always those who read some of their own desires into a new law. They are quite determined that it was passed for their special benefit, and it is not easy to convince them otherwise. There are also those who claim personal friendship with a senator or assemblyman in the hope that this will further their cause.

While relatives and others consistently ask for assistance for the aged, it is less common to have someone urge that aid be granted to a mother and her dependent children. I was rather surprised one morning to get the full treatment from a prominent citizen who insisted that aid be granted a mother and two children. He announced that he was a friend of the senator from our district and the top man in a local lodge. I gave him the usual answer, which was that if she was eligible we would be glad to help her. The usual answer was not good enough for him and he said, "I didn't ask you to find out if she was eligible. I told you to help her."

I repeated that if she was eligible we would see that she received assistance. At this point his tone assumed that of an offened first sergeant in the Marine Corps. "I don't think you understood who I am," he said. "I am R. L. Jay, the grand dragon of the local lodge, and I'm telling you to help this woman!"

It is not the best practice to lose one's composure and answer in kind, but it is not easy to accept an ultimatum to disregard the law either. "Mr. Jay," I replied, "I don't give a damn if you're the Wizard of Oz. If your friend is eligible, she will receive help. If she isn't, she won't." The answer effectively terminated the conversation, but it was not the kind of statement which makes one a leading candidate for membership in the local lodge.

In spite of one's feeling for people resulting from a close association with the poor, there are some things about welfare which are difficult to understand. They are even more difficult to explain to the inquiring public. The legislators and congressmen in their collective wisdom have been concerned about public assistance recipients. In legislating for masses of poor people, they have created some measures which accrue to the advantage of a minority who are dishonest, shiftless and irresponsible.

In the area of honesty, as one looks at the provisions of the welfare code he wonders why any welfare recipients pay their debts and obligations. Those who are dishonest do not, but they constitute a small percentage. In the event a welfare recipient fails or refuses to pay his rent or other obligations, there are no remedies in welfare law to require him to do so. His check cannot be attached or garnisheed. It cannot be held or reduced for his failure to meet his obligations. If he fails to pay his rent, the amount for that item in his budget continues to be paid to him. He can, of course, be taken into court, and a judgment can be entered against him. This, however, is, in most cases, a useless gesture. He has nothing of value which can be attached or seized. The circumstances under which welfare departments can pay his obligations for him are almost nonexistent. The Federal regulations surrounding the so-called money management principle are so complicated and expensive that it is practically impossible to comply with them. The amazing thing is that most welfare recipients are aware of all of this yet continue to live on a marginal existence and pay their debts. One has to conclude that contrary to widespread belief, they must be more honest than the general nonrecipient population.

The matter of welfare grants and wages for unskilled work is a perplexing one. In most of the states the unskilled laborer with a large family can receive a welfare grant when he is unemployed. The amount of welfare aid is often greater than his wage when he is working. This situation sparks an endless debate. Those on one side declare that wages are too low. Those on the other side are convinced that welfare grants are too high. The farm laborer with ten children is in the middle of the controversy. Regardless of how independent and ambitious he may be, he must have mixed feelings about the discontinuance of a $400-a-month welfare grant when he is offered full-time employment for half that figure.

Merchants sometimes complain about welfare recipients who fail to pay their accounts. There are occasions when they have cause to complain. There are times, however when it is difficult to determine why credit was extended in the first place. A local jeweler follows a practice of selling expensive luxury items to welfare recipients. He then complains bitterly to the welfare department when payments are not made. With all the facilities which are available for checking credit ratings, I cannot extend him much sympathy. A large furniture store in our locality seems to specialize in selling furniture to welfare recipients on credit. The firm collects a substantial down payment and a carrying charge. Shortly thereafter, they repossess the furniture. This is repeated over and over with some of the same items. It would appear that the company enters into these transactions with full realization of the final results.

Recently I received a letter from a Hollywood store which specializes in ladies' clothing. It is an exclusive firm and the average working girl cannot afford to purchase her clothing there. The letter listed a number of welfare recipients who were in arrears in their payments. The credit manager who wrote the letter indicated in rather strong terms that this situation was all my fault and that I should do something about it immediately.

The Aid to Totally Disabled law has a provision for attendant home care for those who are unable to care for themselves. This is a wise measure, since it allows the disabled to remain in their own homes rather than to be placed under expensive hospital or nursing home care. Like many good laws it is sometimes subject to misuse. Mrs. R. receives Aid to the Disabled because of her mental condition. She has been an inmate of a mental hospital, but she is harmless and does not need institutional care. To outward appearances she is quite normal. One of her hobbies is visiting numerous doctors' offices. She becomes such a nuisance that some of them give her a harmless prescription to get her on her way.

She became obsessed with the idea that she needed a practical nurse as a combination attendant and housekeeper. She found some difficulty in locating a doctor who would approve this, but one finally wrote such an order. Although there is nothing physically wrong with her, she has her meals prepared, errands run, and house cleaned, and she enjoys the luxuries of manicures and pedicures. The long-suffering taxpayer takes care of all this through his contribution to the welfare department budget.

There are times when objectivity is difficult and when one's thoughts are at considerable variance with his spoken words. Mrs. Jones—or more correctly, Miss Jones—called to complain about the amount of aid her daughter and her daughter's two small minor children were receiving. Mrs. Jones, as she prefers to be called, has never accepted the bonds of matrimony. She has given birth to five children who have five different fathers. The daughter, whose situation she is discussing, is her second born. Her oldest daughter has one illegitimate child. She is living by herself, is unmarried, and is receiving public assistance. The second daughter is now fifteen years of age and has recently given birth to a second illegitimate child.

In the eyes of the law the second daughter is still a child—a sophisticated child in some respects but not yet an adult. As dependent children, she and her babies are considered part of her mother's household. The amount of aid allotted to her and her children is slightly less than it would be if she were living in an independent adult situation.

This has all been explained to Mrs. Jones, and she understands it. She has no inclination to agree with the explanation or to accept it. While her concerns are primarily financial, and our conversation is geared to that level, birth control pills, sterilization and other unmentioned subjects are uppermost in my mind. Not the least of my mental wanderings revolve around the social failures involved. Society in general, and welfare in particular, has tolerated an unfortunate situation which is self-prepetuating. It violates all the cardinal principles of child welfare.

Mrs. Jones is an ardent believer in "states rights." She believes that the state has a right and an obligation to support her and as many of her illegitimate children and grandchildren as may be born.

When situations such as these arise, there are nagging thoughts which plague one's mind and jiggle his conscience. No one wants to discriminate against a helpless child, nor do we want to be termed "blue noses" or "christers." The modern trend of thought is to accept all forms of behavior and to blame society for our failures. Public welfare employees are not legally or officially granted the privilege of passing moral judgments on the behavior of recipients. Perhaps this is the better way; otherwise, someone who is in real need, as well as someone who is floating with the tide, might not reach the shore of public support. Worse than that, some child might go hungry, and there has never been a situation bad enough to justify that.

The time of day and its tempo of complaints and frustrations colors our responses to difficult situations. My conversation with Mrs. Jones occurred near five o'clock after a most trying day. It seemed as if everyone in our community wanted to complain about something on that particular day. Had it happened on a different day, at a different time, my thoughts might have been more tolerant. I doubt, however, that even on the most favorable day I could accept the philosophy that parents have no responsibility for their children and that the omnipotent state is the mother of all of us.

Welfare laws are frequently formulated by politically elected citizens who have had little or no contact with those who dwell in the welfare world. Rules and regulations are all too frequently the product of the minds of office-cloistered maiden ladies. They have never paddled a juvenile bottom in frustration, nor have they had occasion to observe humanity in the raw. Their thoughts cover the ideal situation and the behavior modes of the middle class.

Those who toil in the welfare vineyards rejoice when the legislature adjourns. They give thanks when the rules and regulations are filed on the shelf of inactivity. Like all the rest of humanity, they consciously and unconsciously resist change. In public welfare, however, change by law or regulation is the order of the day.

Chapter X

When Will It All End?

A PROMINENT INDUSTRIALIST is a frequent caller at our department. He has a real concern about rising welfare costs. He begins his conversation with a question and ends it on the same note. He asks if our department is still spending all of his money. We tell him that we are spending a lot of his tax money but that defense and education are spending much more than we are. After we have discussed welfare's problems, he closes his part of the conversation by asking, "When will it all end?"

The last time he called he did not terminate with the familiar question but continued on to discuss a family problem. "I have an old aunt," he said. "She used to be well off, but she has spent all of her money. I want to bring her to the welfare department so she can apply for the Old Age pension. How long will it take?"

I told him that it should not take very long and that I could now answer the question which he always asked. "You asked me when this will all end," I said. "I can now tell you that it will begin to end when people like you begin taking care of their aged aunts."

This answer, of course, was only a partial remedy for a host of social and economic ills which spawn the need for public assistance. It is not at all likely that this generation will see the end of or even a decline in the need for public aid. In fact, given a continuation of the present social, economic and political climate, the need for public assistance in some form will continue to increase.

America has experienced many drastic changes in its patterns of living since the turn of the century. Not the least of these have been social and economic changes, which have given rise to an increasing need for public welfare. Our population has increased

106

disproportionately at the extremities of youth and old age. We have more minor children and more aged people. They represent a much greater percentage of our total population than they did at the close of the last century. Minor children and aged people are not productive segments of our population. They must be supported by the efforts of the labor force, represented by those who are in the prime of their working years.

We have witnessed a revolution in mechanization and a resultant decline in the demand for unskilled labor. Educational requirements have increased, accompanied by a discouraging increase in the numbers of those who fail to complete high school.

Accompanying all the other drastic social and economic changes has been a growing indifference in our personal concern for our needy relatives. This century has witnessed a growing tendency of turning to distant centers of government for services and for aid for our relatives.

The changes in our cultural and economic patterns resemble the tributaries of a great river. As they have combined, there has been a flood tide of need for those caught up in currents which they could not successfully combat. Public welfare has been at the delta of this flood tide and has caught the wreckage of human endeavor which has fallen victim to the volume and pace of social change.

Our efforts at stemming this deluge of problems have consisted largely of expanded and increased public assistance programs. We have done little or nothing to dam the tributaries from which the problems accumulate. We have complained about increasing welfare costs without realizing the changes in our social and economic life which were causing them.

Gainful employment is generally considered to be the antidote for public welfare. As with most of the simple solutions which are suggested to solve complicated problems, it is at best only a partial answer to vexing problems. Employment is related to welfare and the future of one is somewhat allied to trends in the other.

The man who attempts to chart the future trends of welfare and unemployment in our society is undertaking a hazardous task. In 1935, Franklin Delano Roosevelt, as he signed the historic Social Security Act, predicted to those around him, "I can now

see the end of public assistance in America." At the time of his
death in 1945, public assistance was still a thriving and growing
function of local, state and Federal government, and were he still
alive he would witness the spectacle of 8.25 million Americans
who are recipients of public assistance. Add to this number those
receiving unemployment insurance benefits, Social Security, veterans' pensions, Railroad Retirement and other retirement plans,
and we see the employed person at the apex of a reverse triangle
with a heavy load resting upon him. One prediction which can
be safely made is that the apex of the triangle will become smaller
and narrower and that the load upon the employed person will
become heavier. How heavy this load can become before it is
unsupportable is a question which we will have to leave to future
economists and social planners.

If we look at the world situation, we know that by 1980, 80 per
cent of the world's population will be in those nations whose citizens are not producing sufficiently for their basic needs and who
lack adequate food, clothing and shelter. They are the nations
whose people are, even today, hungry and restless.

It might be well at this point to attempt to define unemployment
as it is statistically reported, to measure its present impact on
public welfare, to determine its impact on future welfare trends,
and finally to attempt to predict the direction and volume of public welfare in the years to come.

The term *unemployment* as it is statistically tabulated and reported means different things to different people and in a final
critical analysis means very little of anything which is helpful in
constructive thinking about productive manpower and public
dependency. Unemployment as it is quoted to us considers only
those "in the labor force who are out of work and are actively
seeking employment." This definition is a very narrow one in many
respects. All too frequently its measurements are confined to those
who are drawing unemployment compensation from the local
public employment office and who are registered for work there.
It does not include the countless thousands of individuals who
seek employment entirely on their own, through friends and
acquaintances or private employment agencies. Obviously, the

published figures on unemployment do not present a true and accurate picture of those who are unemployed.

It might well be asked at this time: What is the labor force and who are those who are *actively* seeking work? Is the housewife who works occasionally to supplement the family income a member of the labor force? Is the college student who works weekends, holidays and vacations considered a part of the labor force? What about the over-sixty-five man or woman still actively and gainfully employed? What is the status of the mother of dependent children who, according to law, is required to have "a plan for self-support" but who is frequently unprepared for any kind of gainful employment because of lack of skills, education and motivation? In what category do other unemployable persons fall—those who may be willing but whom no employer will hire?

These are interesting and challenging questions. They are posed to demonstrate the dearth of real information we have about employment and the haziness of the oft-used term *labor force*. Regardless of these gaps in specific knowledge, we must work with what we have available, but at the same time we must be cognizant of the fact that no realistic appraisal of our employment and unemployment picture can be made until we have accurate and working definitions of *employment, unemployment* and *the labor force*.

Even with the sketchy information which is available, the point of time in which we look at unemployment is of extreme importance. The present picture is out of focus because we are in a period of inflation and are engaged in a costly war of indefinite duration. In a war and inflation economy, the unskilled and marginal worker who would be considered unemployable in times of normal economic activity is in demand in spite of his deficiencies and the unproductive economics of his employment.

At the present time, America is enjoying a period of unprecedented prosperity. Our rate of unemployment is approximately 4 per cent of the labor force. Since there is no history of unemployment lower than 3 per cent without serious inflation, it is reasonable to expect that we have reached at least a temporary plateau of so-called full employment. Our gross national product is at an all-time high and indications are that it will continue to grow and increase. As we observe the growth in population and gross national product and the decrease in unemployment, we must also take note of a somewhat puzzling and spectacular growth in public welfare, both in the number of recipients and the amount of funds expended. In California, for instance, since 1961 population has increased by some 15.7 per cent and unemployment has decreased from 7 per cent to 5.8 per cent, while welfare expenditures have increased by more than 70 per cent.

This is a confusing picture and it is evident that there are some things wrong with it. One of these is that our determination of what constitutes the labor force excludes the majority of individuals who are recipients of public assistance. From this we must conclude either that our definition of the labor force is misleading or that the majority of our welfare recipients are unemployable and not properly a part of the labor force. The most honest conclusion probably lies somewhere between the either-or concept with the final conclusion that today unemployment per se is not as influential in determining the course of welfare as we have thought.

Forty per cent of all welfare recipients are aged, blind or disabled; they receive 60 per cent of all welfare expenditures. The balance of recipients are either dependent children under the age of eighteen years, or their parents or caretakers. Subtracting the number of children leaves a comparatively small number and percentage of divorced or deserted mothers and unemployed fathers who are the only welfare recipients available for employment. The majority of this "available" group are questionable prospects for participation as employees in an industrialized society. The mothers by and large are uneducated and unskilled. They have a history of early marriage and some scattered work experience of an unskilled nature performed during their youth. Many of them have physical and emotional health problems which are not conducive to the performance of regular employment, and others have young children who require either the mother's supervision or that of a baby-sitter. To anyone who has observed this group over a period of years, its members do not constitute a promising reservoir of employable persons. Welfare administrators estimate that a maximum of 10 per cent of this group can be trained for, and placed in, full-time gainful employment. This estimate, of course, presumes that the demand for skilled and semiskilled labor will remain at its present peak.

The unemployed fathers receiving public assistance for minor children also present a cheerless picture as far as modern employment demands are concerned. Most of them have had no work experience other than unskilled manual labor. The majority of them have little or no formal education. There is also the man of high skill and limited funds whose skills have become obsolete. He may not be capable of retraining or upgrading.

In the current debate about unemployment and poverty, automation is often termed the sole cause. Much of what we have blamed on automation is more a product of social and economic change, such as the presence of more older people and younger people in our population and the discrimination against older workers, Negroes and other minority groups. There has also been a lack of demand for unskilled and semiskilled labor.

One in three of our low-income families is headed by a person sixty-five years of age or older. Many of the aged and sick are disabled, and many are involuntarily retired. With the high birth rates of the 1940's and 1950's, and with one youth out of four dropping out of high school, we have an increase in young men who have looked for a job and have never found one.

There was a time when our economy needed the unskilled worker, the marginal employee and even the aged person who was still well enough to work. This is a part of our past history which will not be repeated, and technology and automation are rapidly adding to our pool of unemployable persons.

It would appear, therefore, that unemployability is a much more important factor in welfare trends than is unemployment in its narrow sense. In looking at the future of unemployment and welfare we must conclude that unemployment, largely due to unemployability, will increase and that a larger and larger percentage of our population will not be productively employed. As a companion to this trend we must expect that a smaller and smaller percentage of the population will be supporting a larger and larger percentage of our population. It is not too unreasonable to expect that in the next decade one fourth of our population will be nonproductive and will be dependent upon public programs for support.

More than three fourths of our dependent children on welfare rolls across the country are recipients of aid as a result of the divorce or desertion of a parent, usually desertion and usually the father. Desertion—which is described as the "poor man's divorce" —is increasing, and all indications are that it will increase in the foreseeable future. Neither law enforcement nor marriage counseling appears to be able to make any appreciable progress in stemming the tide of desertion. This alone will call for continuing increases in aid to dependent minor children. We have not reached nor will we reach the stage where we will permit minor children to be deprived of the necessities of life. Having failed as a society to assure them parental support we must assume the responsibility for providing public support.

Our aged population is now 8 per cent of our total population. With increasing medical knowledge and skills our aged are increasing in numbers and in percentage and by 1980 will constitute 10 per cent of our population. Many of them are living longer but they are not well and require expensive nursing home and hospital care. The most ardent conservative politician constantly reminds us of our obligations to care for the aged, and we can expect in the future that in addition to an increase in numbers, we can anticipate continuing increases in the cost of caring for aged people. We cannot expect the return of the "good old days," when care of the aged was assumed by relatives. It is now an obligation of government and will continue to be so.

As we move more and more towards an automated economy our basic requirements for education will increase. At the present time the absolute basic educational floor for the overwhelming majority of jobs in our society is graduation from high school. The time is not too far distant when a college degree or some form of highly specialized training will be required to enter the employment market. The discouraging aspect of this trend is that educators tell us that the dropout rate of those who fail to complete high school is actually increasing. It requires no crystal ball to predict that barring unusual circumstances, the high school dropout of today will be applying for public assistance tomorrow. If present trends continue, those who lack the necessary educational requirements will in the future add to the rolls of the unemployable.

Those who are unfortunate in that they are mentally, emotionally or physically ill and crippled have always been with us. Although industrial accidents have decreased, automobile accidents which result in crippling injuries are increasing at an alarming rate. Science and medicine are preventing injuries at birth and childhood influences which stunt and warp mental development, but our highly complex and mobile society continues to spawn an increasing number of emotionally and mentally ill persons. We do not appear at present to have the resources available to alter this trend. Unfortunate relatives of a generation ago were mostly an individual family responsibility, but this has also become an obligation of government, and the mentally and physically handicapped will continue to add their names to the list of unemployables.

In viewing all this, there is a preponderance of evidence that the real labor force will continue to constitute a progressively smaller percentage of our population and those who must look to others for financial support will increasingly become a larger percentage of our population. It follows then that either public welfare or some other system will have to be responsible for an increasing number of individuals. Whether this will be welfare or some other form of public assistance is open to conjecture.

There are some prospects of slowing down the increasing number of dependent persons in the future. They are, however, comparatively new and untried and at best do not have the ultimate answers to the problems which perpetuate dependency. One of these is the matter of birth control. There are good indications that a majority of unskilled and uneducated persons who have large families would limit the number of children if they had adequate birth control information and supplies. This is one ray of hope, but experience alone will determine its effect.

It would be difficult to find very many people today who are happy with the *status quo* of public welfare. The recipients are not happy; they want more money. Those who apply and are rejected are most unhappy. The taxpayer considers it an expensive nightmare which he would like to see disappear with the dawn. Welfare administrators who toil in the paper-ridden jungle of complex regulation would like to see constructive administrative changes, and bureaucrats and self-styled liberals would like to see welfare liberalized and expanded.

This general attitude of unhappiness has produced many suggested changes ranging from complete abolition of welfare to the establishment of family allowance or negative income tax plans. There have also been suggestions that the so-called means test be abolished and that people be assisted if and when they say they need help. There are undoubtedly better ways of assisting some people than through the traditional welfare approach but the "new" plans which have been advanced are also fraught with serious problems.

The obligation of government to help older people has been firmly established in our society. Our efforts and attentions, therefore, should be directed towards the best and most economical system to accomplish this objective. It is evident that public welfare is not the best plan to carry out our obligations to the aged. Assistance to this group at the present time, like many of our other endeavors, is a combination of confusion, duplication and divided responsibility. It ranges from Old Age Assistance and Social Security to housing subsidies, veterans' pensions, and free fishing licenses. In the interests of simplicity, administrative economy and preservation of the dignity of the aged person, it would be proper to expand and increase the involuntary contribution system as represented by Social Security and to make Social Security benefits *the* program for care of the aged. There are other improvements and programs which could replace in a more efficient manner some of the other features of today's current welfare programs.

It might be well to examine briefly the proposed family allowance plan, the negative income tax proposal, and the War on Poverty.

The family allowance plan proposes a monthly payment to all persons below a certain income level based on the number of persons in the family. A variation of the plan is to ignore income and to provide an allowance to everyone regardless of need. This plan on a modified and limited allowance basis is in effect in Canada and some other nations of the world.

The negative income tax plan would set a figure for earnings which would result in those whose incomes were above a set amount paying an income tax and those who had no income or whose incomes were below the basic figure receiving payment from the government.

Both of these plans constitute a simple system of getting money to people. Contrary to the claims of some of their supporters, they do set a "means test" figure. The magic figure where poverty ends and affluence begins constitutes a means test regardless of where it is set. They ignore fundamental principles of human nature and human behavior and could have disastrous social consequences. It has been said that useful work is the salvation of the human race and that mass unemployment continued over a period of time would result in mass mental illness. Both of these plans place a premium on unemployment or underemployment and lack a stress on the dignity and benefits of labor which have been cornerstones in the foundations of our ordered society. It is likely that under these proposed systems the majority of people would prefer to be employed, but it is a fact of life that there are some individuals who would prefer not to work, and these systems would favor those persons.

It is conceivable that with family example being dominant in the formation of character and personality, we could in the course of a few generations produce a shiftless and irresponsible society. One of the most serious effects of welfare has been the deterioration of family life of those on public assistance. While welfare recipients have been provided with necessities, they have dropped out of the mainstream of American life. With the regular receipt of a subsistence check has come discouragement, lack of purpose, and a disordered way of life. Gone is the system and regularity of a home where there is a breadwinner. Gone also is the example of the head of the household who toils in order that the family may have the necessities and comforts of life. The economics of these plans are open to question but their potential social impact presents even a much more serious problem. With all of the criticism of the "giveaway" welfare programs it is difficult to conceive of the American public embracing either a family allowance or a negative income tax plan.

In the event that our nation should move in this direction or even with increased numbers of welfare recipients under the present system it would seem imperative that we institute some kind of public works program. Although the old Work Projects Administration program was the beneficiary of much ridicule it was in many ways superior to our present welfare programs for unemployed persons. In the future an increasing number of unemployable persons may have to receive their support from government, but a useful public works program which would employ them would prevent to some extent a deterioration otherwise in moral fiber and work habits generated by plans which put a premium on idleness.

The antipoverty program has been honeycombed with partisan politics and riddled with incompetent and impractical administration. It has been expected to accomplish the elimination of poverty in the span of a few months and with the expenditure of a billion dollars. It is generally recognized by realistic students of our economic and social structure that we will always have some poverty with us. A substantial reduction in its occurrence will require a generation of intelligent planning and the expenditure of many billions of dollars. Perhaps a generation will have to elapse before we can achieve tangible results in the poverty war and consequently ease the welfare burden. Our best hope is that the next adult generation, now in the lower school grades, will not repeat the pattern of their parents, many of whom are physically able but totally unequipped for productive employment in a modern industrial world.

If we were seriously concerned about the mere elimination of poverty, we could, with an annual appropriation of some 30 billion dollars, guarantee an adequate income to everyone in the United States. The social and psychological results might well be catastrophic, but if we are looking for a one-shot, patent-medicine remedy for poverty, this is it.

Finally, an objective study of our social and economic structure and a consideration of present and future trends in unemployment and welfare should convince us that there is no easy road to recovery from our present situation and that there will, in the future, be continuing increases in unemployment and in some form of welfare.

We should level our best efforts and our most imaginative minds to the elimination of those conditions which are conducive to dependency and which will stimulate a productive society. At the same time we must accept the fact that we will continue to have in our society those individuals who are not capable of dealing with its frustrations and its complexities. Realizing this, we need to establish those programs and systems which will provide for the unfortunate and the inadequate in the most humane and economical manner possible.